May 7, 1989

To Janine

L__ & Best Wishes

& – Aunt Lil

52
STORIES
and
POEMS
for
CHILDREN

52
STORIES
and
POEMS
for
CHILDREN

Illustrated by Margery Wind

Publishing House
St. Louis

1   2   3   4   5   6   7   8   9   10   MAL   96   95   94   93   92   91   90   89   88   87

CONTENTS

The Peculiar Pumpkin Seed

by Karen Bigler

Brent planted a pumpkin seed in a milk carton full of dirt, patted it, watered it, and put it on the windowsill next to his bed. Brent had a very special bed. You see, his daddy made a special frame out of wood so Brent's bed could be up high and he could play below during the day.

Oh, what fun Brent had! Sometimes his bed was a ship and he was the captain sailing across the sea. Or, other times his bed was a covered wagon which was captured and surrounded by wild Indians.

Now, every night Brent would say his prayers, kiss his mom and dad good night, and climb up the ladder to his bed. Before pulling up his covers, he would look at the dirt in his milk carton. He took his magnifying glass and looked hard for the first sign of a green stem. Nothing!

"Oh, Mom, when will my pumpkin seed begin to grow? I water it each morning and I give it good light by the window. I hope I have the biggest pumpkin in the whole neighborhood for Halloween."

Brent's mom kissed him again and said, "Just be patient, Brent. God plans all things with perfect timing—even a small seed and when it should grow."

Brent laid his head back on his pillow. Oh how tired he was! It had been a busy day.

No sooner had his eyelids closed than he pictured a tiny green stem pushing its way up through the soft brown dirt. It grew and grew and pushed its way out the window and across the front yard. The stem was as big and round as the trunks of the fir trees in Brent's yard. Giant leaves were everywhere. The stem grew across the road and the vines covered the entire neighborhood. It looked like a

1

jungle outside. Orange blossoms burst from the stems everywhere and then popped into small green pumpkins. All of a sudden, the little, hard green balls began to grow— like green balloons being blown up with air. They grew bigger . . . and bigger . . . and BIGGER . . . until they were as big as giant beach balls! The sun started to rise and turned them into a fiery bright orange color.

Now that it was morning, people were waking up and gasping as they opened their doors. The vines had grown everywhere and completely blocked the street. The people couldn't get out of their houses to get the morning newspaper. Moms and dads couldn't drive to work. The school bus couldn't get through to pick up the children for school. The mailman couldn't deliver the letters and packages.

Everyone was angry and upset. The grown-ups chopped at the vines, trying to clear a pathway for their cars so they would not be late for work. The children, however, squealed with delight to see so many pumpkins . . . like seeing the first fallen snow. They ran around tearing off the pumpkins and rolling them into a pile that looked like a mountain. Suddenly, one little boy grabbed a pumpkin from beneath the pile and they all began to roll . . . like lava overflowing a volcano. They rolled and rolled and crashed and crashed with a terrific thundering sound . . . and made a pathway down the entire road.

Everyone screamed with joy, "Hurray! Hurray!"

This woke Brent from his dream. He sat straight up in his bed and opened his eyes . . . only to find himself sitting in his room and not in a jungle of vines. He quickly crawled to the window and gazed at his milk carton of dirt. There in the center of the dark brown soil was a very tiny green stem peeking up at Brent.

"Praise God," Brent shouted as he ran down the stairs to show his mom and dad. His pumpkin seed had finally begun to grow!

My Dearest Friend

by Gloria A. Truitt

Each time I need a loving friend
to keep me company,
I always choose that Someone, who
will stay right next to me.
And when I need a caring friend
to help me with a task,
I never hesitate at all;
I know the One to ask.
When I am feeling frightened, or
when I am feeling sad,
I call upon my dearest Friend;
then nothing seems that bad.
My Friend can be your best Friend, too—
trust His loving care;
For Jesus died and rose for us,
and He is *everywhere*!

Little Sister

by Tellie Hart

Rachel swung slowly. Her sandals dragged in the small hole formed under the wooden swing. The servants had hung the swing on the fig tree in the courtyard.

Voices around the yard disturbed her. Women stood in groups talking soberly, often looking over their shoulders to where she was swinging. She could hear Aunt Abigail's shrill voice from inside the house instructing the servants.

Earlier her aunt had yelled at her, "Rachel, you just get out from underfoot! With sickness in this house, we surely don't need a noisy little girl around."

"I'm not a little girl," Rachel had burst out. "I'm almost nine!"

For a moment Rachel had feared that Aunt Abigail might strike her. She had towered over the child, her eyes snapping in anger. "You heard what I said, young lady! It's your fault that Ruth is sick, anyway. You insisted on going out to the hills for a picnic. She only went to please you. That sudden storm soaked both of you. It's a wonder you aren't sick, too. That's all we need!"

Rachel had escaped to the swing out in the courtyard. She flew high in the tree, disturbing birds in their nests. At the very top she could see the dome of the synagog in Capernaum. Her father was one of the rulers there. He sat in the circle of men on the main floor. He often read from the Scriptures, and Rachel loved to hear his voice as she peeked through the lattice that separated the men and boys from the women and girls.

She could almost hear her father's deep voice now. "A man must be ruler over his own house before he is fit to rule the people."

Rachel shivered. If Aunt Abigail told him of his small daughter's impertinence, she knew what he'd say. "The sin of rebellion is the same as witchcraft, and God hates it." She should not have talked back to her aunt.

Still, a little sister was capable of worry, too. Why was Ruth always so sick? Everyone knew she had never been strong. Long ago Rachel had overheard the physician talking to her father. "She will never be hearty and strong, Jairus; not like your younger one." He chuckled and rubbed his beard. "That one is full of life and energy. Only God knows why there is such a difference."

Suddenly the voices around her rose. In the hubbub, Rachel saw her father hurry from the house and out the gate. A crowd followed him. Rachel joined them, slipping between two women so Aunt Abigail could not see her from the house.

"This is no time to leave," complained one. "When his daughter is on the brink of death, you would think he would stay beside her."

"Where is he going?" demanded another.

"I think he's going for that carpenter, the Healer."

Rachel stubbed her toe and almost fell. Her heart was heavy. Why would her father hunt for a carpenter when Ruth was so sick? Was he going to have a coffin made? Rachel shuddered.

A man stumbled over her. "Go home, little girl. You're in the way. This is no place for you."

Many people joined the crowd as it passed, but now suddenly they all stopped. Something was happening ahead, but no one could see. Some stood on tiptoe, grumbling and complaining about the crowd.

Suddenly the people parted. An older woman was coming toward them, her arms upraised. Tears were streaming down her face.

"I touched Him!" she cried joyfully. "I touched Him!"

5

As everyone turned to watch the woman depart, Rachel saw an opening and scurried through it. She rushed ahead, then stopped at the sight of her father. He was on his knees on the ground in front of a man. Several other men stood protectively around them. Rachel watched in horror. Her father, ruler of the synagog, groveling in the dust before this man!

As the men turned her way, Rachel slipped back into the crowd. She did not want to be seen. She could see that they were heading for her home, her father leading them. She stared at the tall man as He passed her. Yes, that would be Jesus! She had seen Him before. Ruth had told her that this man was able to cure cripples and sick people.

Rachel hung back. She did not want to get too close. It would not do for her father to discover her. They were almost at the gate to her house when she heard a high pitched wail that rent the air.

A cold chill ran down Rachel's back. She had heard that sound before. It always meant someone was dead. Dead? Who? Oh, no! Not Ruth!

A sob caught in Rachel's throat as she pushed and shoved to get inside her own home. The wailing hurt her eardrums. Her heart was pounding with fear.

Suddenly the wailing stopped. The silence was more fearful than the wailing. Then the crowd began laughing.

"Did you hear that?" laughed a man. "He said she was not dead but sleeping. Imagine that! Sleeping, he says!"

There! She was inside now. Where was her father? Where was that man called Jesus? Rachel rushed toward the kitchen. Strong arms grasped her. It was Aunt Abigail.

Her eyes were red from weeping. "Oh, you poor baby," she crooned. "No, Rachel, Jesus gave strict instructions that no one was to follow. Only your mother and father, and several of His men were permitted to go into Ruth's room. Come, Child. We can sit in here with the other women."

She drew Rachel across the hall. Rachel moved obediently, relieved that her aunt seemed to have forgotten her previous behavior. In the crowded room women were talking softly, some wiping their eyes.

"Aunt Abigail," whispered Rachel. "I'm so tired. Can I go up to my room and lie down?"

Her aunt patted Rachel's cheek. "Oh, you poor darling. Everyone has forgotten about you. I know you must be worn out, too. Yes, go to your room and take a nap. You need it."

At the doorway to her room, Rachel paused. The whole house wore an expectant hush. She could hear a murmur of voices coming from her sister's room. Rachel tiptoed down the hall to listen at the closed door.

She was startled when the door suddenly opened. Rachel moved back quickly. Behind the men coming out, she saw Ruth sitting up in bed. Mother was crying. Her father sat in a chair, his face buried in his hands.

Rachel wanted to rush inside, but something made her turn toward her own room. A hand on her shoulder stopped her. She looked up into the dark eyes of the man called Jesus. He squatted down in front of her so that their eyes were level.

He smiled as He spoke. He could not miss the trembling of the little girl's lips. "Child, your sister is all right now. Will you please do something for Me? Will you go downstairs and tell someone to bring your sister something to eat?"

A man behind Him looked down with a smile, too. He nodded his head.

Rachel felt as if her heart might burst. This man had saved her sister! With a little sob, she threw herself into His arms.

Allison Meets Professor Feathertuft

by Winifred Rouse Simpson

The late afternoon was swimming with sunshine. Allison was helping her brother, Tad, fill large flower pots with rich black dirt. Then Mother could plant bright red geraniums on the porch.

"We need another pot, Sugar," said Tad.

"I'll get it," said Allison. She dashed around the corner, then stopped.

The shed door stood gaping like the wide mouth to a deep cave. Inside it was dark, cool, and musty smelling. Her heart thumped and her stomach fluttered. Just as she reached for the pot on the shelf above her head, Allison thought she saw tiny eyes glowing. She gave a little gasp—the small sort of sound one makes when stung by a bee—and stepped back.

All at once the heavy pot toppled from the shelf and bonked Allison's head with a *THWACK!* Brightly colored lights wheeled before her eyes and everything turned very black.

"Gracious! Are you all right?" asked a soft furry voice.

"I . . . I think so," answered Allison opening her eyes. To her surprise she saw a fat lady raccoon sitting at the door.

Allison blinked. "Who are you?" she asked quietly.

"I'm Pennywaddle," said the raccoon. "That was a rather nasty rap you took. I'd better have a look."

Allison crawled out of the shed and sat on the damp grass. Tiny fingers probed into her long hair and gently touched the bump on her head. "OUCH!" cried Allison.

"Just as I thought," said Pennywaddle. "Come along, Dear."

"Come where?" asked Allison as the raccoon wiggled toward the lilac hedge.

"Why, home," she answered. "A good herb tea is just the thing for head lumps. Take care, as we don't want another!"

Allison crawled toward the hedge, but stopped when she saw Pennywaddle disappear into a dark drainage pipe.

"I can't go in there? I can't! I won't," she panted.

Pennywaddle backed out of the pipe and sat down. "But it *IS* the shortest way, you know. And I'll be with you."

"Oh, you don't understand. I ... I can't," wailed Allison.

The raccoon sniffed Allison's face and licked a salty bead of sweat from her forehead. "No, of course you can't," she said gently. "We'll just take the long way round."

It took about an hour to go through the woods because Pennywaddle kept finding dark little thickets which needed looking into. At last she called, "Here we are," and squeezed into a dense patch of ivy and tangled roots.

There was one rather bad moment for Allison when the shadows became very thick; she swallowed hard several times. But then she came out into a large cave with the floor swept smooth and a cheery fire crackling on a stone hearth. Six children were busy with chores and, being curious like all children, kept peeking shyly at Allison.

Pennywaddle drew chairs around a long wooden table and called, "Wake up, Professor! I'm pouring out the tea."

"Tu-whoo, shoo!" said a sleepy voice above Allison.

"Oh, it's an owl," she cried, glancing up at a bundle of white fluffy feathers perched on a high shelf next to a clock.

"What's the to-do?" said the Owl, taking his head out from under his wing and opening one eye. "Tea? Tu-whoo!"

9

And with a whirr of his wings he joined them at the table. He was quite the largest owl Allison had ever seen.

Allison was delighted with the spread of nuts and fruit. The hot cinnamon herb tea was very refreshing as well. At last, when each person had finished his (or her) meal with a long sigh of contentment, Pennywaddle made the introductions.

"The children go by numbers and this is Professor Feathertuft," she said nudging him. "We have a stranger."

"Ranger! Where?" he said, twisting his head about to inspect the cave. "I don't see a ranger, Tu-whoo."

"Do forgive the Professor as he's still not fully awake," she said. Pennywaddle spoke into his ear. "The girl is Allison."

"The girls are all sons?" said the Owl. "I don't believe a word of it! Not true; not true! Tu-whoo!"

"Allison! She's afraid of the dark," yelled Pennywaddle.

"Lark?" hooted the Professor. "Lark's call the morning, night-hunter's warning. Nightingale's call, thrill to all!"

Pennywaddle shook herself until the tip of her tail frizzed. "Not lark. DARK!" she shouted.

"There's no need to shout," said Professor Feathertuft, blinking. "Dark is soft and friendly."

"Not to me," admitted Allison. "I can't see in the dark and something might be waiting to pounce on me."

"Tu-whoo, true! But, being wise, I know dark is friendly. I'm not a mere chick, you know. I've spread a wing or two in my time. Fear is friendly, too!" he announced quite firmly.

Pennywaddle patted Allison's hand. "That's right, Dear. Feathertuft's a wise old bird, and I listen to his counsel."

Allison shook her head. "Daytime is better for me. And who says dark is friendly anyway?"

10

"HE said! Tu-whoo."

"Who? Who is *he*?" asked Allison.

"Are you teasing me?" he asked sternly. "*HE*! The Master. God. He made the dark and said it was good. So it is, tu-true! Dark is a friendly time for hunting. If I didn't hunt, the world would be overrun with bats and moths and not very nice things. Dark is friendly to humans, tu-whoo! It is a quiet time for resting. Saves the eyes from all that glare."

Allison thought that was a very extraordinary way to look at the dark. But she didn't agree with him about fear and told the Professor so very plainly.

"To *NOT* fear is foolish!" he cried. "A healthy fear makes you careful, and careful makes you safe. Everyone has a fear! Too-whooo!"

"Gracious yes," agreed Pennywaddle. "Why, if I didn't teach the children fear, Number One would have made a nice dinner for Ruddy Foxfrazzle. And Number Four has a bad habit of getting too near roads. Why, the way those gas-o-mobiles tear about, laying waste to the land, he would have been flat long ago." Glancing at the clock, she added, "It's time for you to leave, Allison. I'm ever so glad you could visit. Just hop on the Professor's back and he'll whisk you home."

Allison thanked Pennywaddle for the lovely tea and climbed onto Professor Feathertuft's back. His feathers were beautifully warm, and soon she was gliding through the trees with a gentle wind in her face.

His landing was a bit rough though—Allison wondered later if she had been too heavy for him—and as she tumbled off his back, her head met the corner of the shed smartly.

I'm sure you know how it is when you have a sore finger and you're always bumping the same spot over and over again. This is what happened to Allison and she bruised the very same lump which the flower pot had made

11

on her head. She became woozy, and when she opened her eyes Tad was staring down at her with a very concerned look.

"Glory, Sis!" he said tenderly. "Are you okay?"

"Yes!" she cried, flinging her arms about his neck. "I had a lovely tea with Pennywaddle, and the Professor flew me home on his back. They told me all about the friendly dark, and how it's okay to be afraid of things sometimes."

Tad looked as though he didn't believe her. He was at that awkward beginning-adult age. (And you know how some adults won't believe something terrific unless it happens to them.) But he had the good grace not to say so out loud. Instead, he told her "Everyone's afraid sometimes," and Allison told him, "That's what Professor Feathertuft told me"; and then they both agreed she had a nasty lump on her head.

That night Allison sat by her window for a long time. God made so many things for her to enjoy, maybe she could learn to like the friendly darkness too. Then she prayed: "Thank You, God, for the beautiful day, for summer sun and happy play. Thank You for dark when the day is done, and for Jesus, my Savior, Your only Son, Amen." She was almost asleep when Professor Feathertuft called from the maple tree and reminded her to climb into bed. He was half hidden by the broad leaves, but Allison was certain that he winked.

"Good-night, Professor," she whispered. "Good hunting."

12

Quacky Finds a Home

by Gloria A. Truitt

"Mother! Look what I have! My very own duck!" yelled Laura as she bounded into the kitchen carrying a large cardboard box.

"A duck?" said Mother. "Where did you ever find it? We're several blocks from the lake."

"I found Quacky in the school yard," explained Laura, "just waddling along beside the fence."

Although Mother was not an expert on ducks, she quickly examined Quacky and decided that one of its wings must have been injured. "When someone can easily pick up a wild creature, Laura, something must be wrong with it. I think we should take it to the Veterinary Clinic."

As Mother drove to the clinic, Laura peeked into the box. "She's not hungry, Mother," said Laura sadly. "She hasn't touched the bread we gave her." The duck lay cuddled in a corner of the box as if sleeping, her beak nestled in the soft feathers of her neck. The only sign of life was the slow in-and-out movement of her breathing.

As Mother and Laura sat in the clinic's waiting room, Laura looked around, smiling at the other animals. Across the room a toy poodle sat trembling on a man's lap. Over in a corner a young lady held a baby skunk. The lady smiled at Laura and asked, "What do you have in the box?"

"Quacky—my very own duck," answered Laura. "I just found her."

A moment later Mrs. Schaefer, a friend of Mother's, arrived with a large metal suitcase. At the end was a square of wire screening. A tiny face appeared at the screen and meowed. "Oh, how cute!" exclaimed Laura as she bent over to say hello to the friendly kitten.

Soon Dr. Baker invited Mother, Laura, and Quacky into the examining room. "Well, what do we have here?" asked Dr. Baker as he lifted Quacky from the box.

Laura explained the whole story while Dr. Baker examined Quacky. He was very kind and treated her gently. "Her wings seem to be just fine," he said. "This kind of duck is called a merganser. But the mystery is, how did she become lost in a school yard? She's confused and frightened because she's away from her natural environment," explained Dr. Baker. "If you try to keep her, Laura, I'm afraid she will soon die."

"Even if we put her in a big wire pen with a plastic pool?" Laura asked hopefully.

Dr. Baker slowly shook his head. "I know you would like to keep her, but she is a wild duck and should be set free."

After Mother and Laura had thanked Dr. Baker, they put Quacky back in the box and drove home.

When Father came home from work, Laura ran to meet him at the door. "Look what we have—a duck! She's mine, but I can't keep her," Laura added sadly. "Would you help us find a safe home for her?"

"She certainly is cute," said Father, "but she's so quiet and still. Is she sick?" Quacky didn't move, not even when Father gently stroked the soft feathers on her back.

"No," Laura sighed, "she's only sad because she's not with other ducks. I asked Dr. Baker if I could keep her, but he said she would die."

"Well," said Father, "there's only one thing for us to do. Jesus teaches us to love and care for each other, and I'm sure He means Quacky, too. We must find a home for her right now."

As Father drove to the edge of town, Mother said, "You know we're doing the right thing, Laura. Don't worry; Quacky will be just fine."

14

Father knew exactly where they should take the little duck. He turned onto a narrow gravel road which led to a smooth, flat bank where a wide, calm river reflected the late afternoon sun from its glassy surface. Here and there, birds darted from the branches overhead, and crickets sang with the frogs that sat hidden in the rushes. In the middle of the river was a small island.

Oh, how beautiful, thought Laura as she gently took Quacky from the box. "Do you think she knows how to swim?" she asked.

"We'll soon see," answered Father as the duck waddled off to the water's edge. As soon as Quacky's webbed feet touched the water, she skimmed off with amazing speed. Immediately she began dipping her beak into the water for food. Quacky circled around just once as if to say good-bye, then swam up the narrow channel on the far side of the island.

"Where did she go?" Laura cried. "I can't see her anymore."

Father and Mother stood quietly with Laura, searching the water in the setting sun, but they couldn't see any sign of Quacky. At last Father took Laura's hand and said, "I think we should go home, Laura, don't you? We must believe that Quacky is happy and safe."

As Laura climbed into the car, a tear trickled down her cheek. "If only I could be sure."

Just as Father started the car's engine, Laura suddenly yelled out, "Look, look! I see Quacky!"

Mother and Father turned to where Laura was pointing. There, swimming around the far end of the island, was a whole flock of ducks. "I wonder which one is ours?" Father exclaimed with a big smile.

"Don't you know?" laughed Laura. "She's the happiest one—the duck who's quacking the loudest."

Rain

by Gloria A. Truitt

Pitter, patter goes the rain,
Tapping on my window pane.
Little rivers running down
To drip upon the thirsty ground.
The sun makes little diamond drops
That sparkle when the shower stops.
And while I watch the rain, I think,
"So that's how God gives earth a drink!"

Faraway Twin

by Lois Zimmermann

"Mama, why are you putting that picture of a little girl on the mantel with Dennis's and mine?"

"Well, Wendy, I've been wanting to talk to you about her, but I waited to receive her picture. It just came today. This girl is a new member of our family, but she lives in another country."

"How can she be in our family if she doesn't even live here? Doesn't she have her own mother and father?"

"Yes, her parents love her and take care of her as best they can. But they need a little help so that she will have enough food and can go to the doctor if she's sick, and so she'll grow up to be healthy and happy, the way you are."

"Doesn't she really have enough to eat? Why doesn't Jesus help her?"

"Don't you see? Jesus is helping her—through us. Haven't I always told you that God loves everybody in the whole world, and He wants us to take care of each other?"

"Yes, but I didn't think we'd take care of someone so far away. Can we go to visit her?"

"Maybe, some day."

"Can she visit us?"

"Perhaps. But, in the meantime, you can send her pictures and cards and tell her about yourself and Dennis. You know, you and Pilar are about the same age."

"Pilar? I've never heard a name like that. And, look— her clothes are funny too. But she is pretty."

"In her country, that's the way children dress. She'd probably think your clothes were funny, too."

"What about Dennis? Will he like having a new sister he can't see?"

"Of course he will—when he's old enough to understand. Then you can tell him about Pilar. Now, you get busy with your crayons and pencil, and we'll get a letter off to her right away."

"Do you think she'll answer it?"

"Of course she will, but it will take a little time because she lives so far away. She'll want to tell you all about herself and her family and her school and church."

"And I can tell her about my school and my Sunday school. And, she'd probably like to hear about Rags, our doggie. Momma, could you send her a picture of Dennis and Rags and me? She'll want to know what her new family looks like."

"As soon as Dennis wakes up from his nap, we'll snap a picture."

"Okay; I'll get my letter ready. But then I want to tell my friends about my new twin sister. Maybe they can have new brothers and sisters, too. I know Marcia would like one. She doesn't have any brothers or sisters at home. I think she'd like to have a brother best because she's a tomboy."

"You may be right, Wendy. Now tell me, how are you going to start your letter?"

"I'm going to ask her if she sings *Jesus Loves Me* in her Sunday school like I do."

Abe's Mashed Potato Mountain to God

by Kevin Gingrich

One day a boy named Abe saw dirt flying out of a hole in the backyard of one of his friends. Abe already knew what it was all about, but he went to see for himself, anyway.

In the backyard he found his three friends, Nick, Morris, and Larry, down in a great big hole. They were very dirty. All three of them had a father's shovel in hand.

"What are you guys doing?" Abe asked, but he knew exactly what they were doing.

"Diggin' a hole to the center of the earth," said Nick. She was a girl. "Go get your dad's shovel."

"Nah-h," said Abe. "I don't want to." The truth was, Abe had tried digging a hole before. It got too hard.

"Watch out, then," said Larry, and a bomb of dirt landed on Abe's new tennis shoes. "We've got lots of work to do."

So Abe left his friends behind—and below—with dirt flying out of the hole as never before.

"We'll get to the center of the earth by suppertime!" they called after Abe. The truth was, their shovels were already scraping the hard earth like spoons scraping on empty plates.

Abe walked home by himself, a bit lonely because his friends weren't with him. Then he began to run.

At home, he got out his baseball and bat. He tossed the ball into the air, and—puff!—he missed it. The ball rolled just beyond his own shadow, which was stretched out on the lawn. He picked up the ball again and—puff!—it rolled right to the long face of his shadow and stopped. He pretended that his shadow's mouth caught the ball. It

19

didn't hurt, though, because a shadow has no teeth. Abe pretended that his shadow was his friend today.

Soon it got too late and too hard for Abe to play baseball, especially by himself. Abe's shadow was getting too big to be a good friend anymore.

"Almost suppertime," grumbled Abe's tummy. Abe pretended that his tummy could talk.

"Those diggers prob'ly aren't to the center of the earth yet," he pretended his tummy said. (Abe pretended that his tummy had said it, because he himself was not supposed to grumble about his friends.)

"But, I bet they have a neat hole," he said. This Abe himself said, but he heard his tummy grumble when he said it.

"You'd better get some supper," Abe told his tummy.

Into the house Abe dragged his tummy, his shadow, and his bat and ball. They all sat down for supper.

"Please put away your bat and ball, Dear," said Abe's mother. Abe put away his bat and ball.

"No food for you tonight," he told his bat and ball. "You can't eat, either," he told his shadow, which had disappeared. "You don't have any teeth."

When Abe sat down again, his mother had a big hill of mashed potatoes piled on his plate. They were potatoes from his dad's garden.

"Thank you, Mother," Abe said.

"You can sit on my lap," he whispered to his grumbling tummy.

Abe's father sat down, too, and he said the blessing. This is what he prayed:

> "Lord, we labor long and hard
> With sweat upon our head;
> But thank You, Lord, for giving us
> This table full of bread.
> In Jesus' name we pray. Amen."

"Please pass the bread," said Abe. His tummy was hungry. His father handed him the bread. Abe liked bread with his potatoes. So did his tummy.

Abe took his bread and folded it like a piece of paper. He had seen his father do this many times. With the bread, Abe began to scoop a great big hole in his potatoes. Abe had never seen his father do this, but he was thinking about the diggers, Nick, Morris, and Larry.

"Please don't play with your potatoes, Dear," his mother told him.

"I'm not," said Abe, and he quickly filled in the hole, making a big pile of potatoes. Picking up his spoon, Abe was about to take a big bite when he got an idea. Yes! The mashed potato mountain gave him a great idea.

"I'll show you," he said.

"Pardon me?" asked his father.

"Oh, no," said Abe. "I was just talking to my tummy."

After supper, Abe took a bath. He took his idea with him to the bath. After the bath, he went to bed, and he took his idea with him when he went to bed.

The only time Abe forgot his idea was when his father came to tuck him in and to pray. This is what his father prayed:

> "Lord, we thank You for the day,
> The many things You've blessed.
> Before the night is gone away,
> We pray You'll give us rest.
> In Jesus' name we pray. Amen."

Abe fell into a deep, deep sleep.

The next morning, Abe woke up. He still had his idea—the mashed potato mountain idea.

After breakfast, Abe ran to the garage to get his dad's shovel. Then he ran into the backyard, into the garden. There he began to dig—and dig, and dig, and dig.

21

When Nick, Morris, and Larry came by, Abe did not ask them if they wanted to help. But, they did not want to help anyway.

"We got in trouble last night," said Morris. "Larry's dad fell in our hole."

"*I* won't get in trouble," Abe told them. "I'm not digging a hole to the center of the earth. I am building a mountain!"

And so he was. Nick, Morris, and Larry watched as Abe flipped dirt out of his hole onto a growing mound. Already, Abe had piled the dirt up as high as his friends' knees. It was the mashed potato mountain made of dirt!

"Where are you building a mountain to?" Nick, Morris, and Larry wanted to know.

"To God," Abe told them. I'm going to climb my mountain to God." This was better than a hole, Abe thought.

When his three friends left, Abe kept digging and digging and digging—and the mountain grew and grew and grew until it was as high as Abe's head. But God still seemed a long way up.

That afternoon, Abe's father came out to the garden. Abe got in trouble, too. He had to put all the dirt back into his hole. But, his father helped him.

Abe was filthy-dirty from all his work, so his daddy took him into the house and washed him up for supper.

After the table prayer and over the mashed potatoes, Abe's father told him something. "You don't have to climb to God," he said, "because God has already came down to you. Remember? Jesus did it."

"Oh, yeah," said Abe as he dug into his mashed potatoes. "I'm glad. I don't think I could have gotten all the way up to Him. Besides, I was getting pretty hungry."

For once, his tummy did not grumble.

Losers Weepers

by Phydella Hogan

Joel screwed on the propeller while his best friend, Brad, glued the tailpiece in place. They stepped back to admire their model plane.

"Joel," called his mother.

"Just a minute, Mom," he replied.

Hastily, he scraped shavings into the wastebasket, gave the propeller an experimental twirl, and headed for the kitchen.

"Isn't she a beauty?" Brad said as they left the workroom. "Now all we have to do is paint her and put on the decals."

"We have to earn money for paint first," answered Joel.

The kitchen smelled of spice and vanilla. His mother lifted a pan of cupcakes from the oven and deftly flipped them onto the table beside several more. Joel reached for them.

"One each," she said. "Those are for the church picnic tonight. I want you to run down to the store and get two pounds of powdered sugar for icing. Here's five dollars—and don't lose the change."

"Can we have an ice cream cone?" asked Joel as he stuffed the money into his pocket.

"May we," corrected his mother. "Yes, but don't dawdle. It's almost five o'clock."

As they hurried up the street, Brad continued to chatter about the plane. It *was* beautiful. And the best part was that they had made it themselves. "Not bad for third-graders," Brad emphasized.

Joel had found the plans in a school book and, together, they had cut their own pattern. They had earned the money for materials by running errands, carrying out trash, and pulling weeds for the neighbors. But the thin balsa wood had split the wrong way, so they'd had to buy more. Now they had no money left to buy paint.

They stopped at the Dairy Bar first and took their place at the end of a long line. Before their turn came, several more people stood in behind them.

"That girl sure is slow," said Brad.

"Must be new. I've never seen her here before," answered Joel.

Finally it was their turn. As the girl began filling their order, a man behind them said, "What's the hold up, Girl? Do you have to make that ice cream?"

The girl blushed, but didn't answer as she thrust two cones at Joel and handed him two quarters and some bills.

Joel stuck the money in his picket, handed Brad a cone, and said, "Now we really have to move it." They hurried on to the store, licking at the ice cream.

At the supermarket they found the sugar and stepped to the checkout counter. Joel swallowed the last of his cone and dug the money from his pocket.

"That will be $1.63," said the clerk.

As he pulled two ones from the crumpled bills, Joel saw a five dollar bill, too. Carefully, he transferred it to another pocket and waited for his change. When they were outside, he asked Brad, "Did you see how much money Mom gave me?"

"No; but she said, 'Here's five dollars and don't lose the change.' Why? Did you lose some?"

Joel pulled out the five. "Then I've got five dollars extra. I still have two ones and some change from Mom's five."

"Whee!" shouted Brad. "Let's go buy that paint!"

"But it's not our money. The girl at the Dairy Bar must have made a mistake."

"Too bad," said Brad. "Finders keepers, losers weepers."

"Except we didn't find it," argued Joel.

"What's the difference? You didn't steal it. If that girl was dumb enough to give it to you, it's not your fault."

"Well, we can't buy paint now, anyway. I have to take this sugar home." Joel still had an uneasy feeling in the back of his mind as he turned into his own yard.

Joel calmly counted the change back to his mother, but he could almost feel the five burning a hole through his pocket. He kept arguing with himself while he helped ice the cupcakes and set the table for supper. At seven, the family left for the picnic. Joel's pocket felt heavy.

There was food galore, and a big crowd was wandering from table to table, sampling it all. Some kids were already playing the games that were set up, and a few were watching or competing in the races. There would be fireworks later.

Joel wandered around, fingering the money in his pocket. He sampled another cupcake, but it didn't taste as good as the one this afternoon.

Was he really stealing, he wondered. Of course not, he told himself. Only he didn't feel quite right. What was it the teacher had said last week at Sunday school? Something about cheating and lying being the same as stealing, and a little sin being as bad as a big one. But he hadn't lied. He just hadn't mentioned it. Twice he had started to tell his mother, but she was busy. Or had he known she'd make him take it back? Oh, pooh, he told himself. That girl probably didn't even miss the money. And if she did, she wouldn't know where it was. Besides, it belonged to the Dairy Bar, not her.

Joel stopped to watch one of the games. Some teenage girls were standing there chattering.

"Sherry got fired at the Dairy Bar tonight," said one.

"Poor Sherry!" said another.

"No wonder!" another chimed in. "She was slow as molasses in January. I thought we'd never get our malts this afternoon."

"That wasn't the reason," said the first girl. "Her register was short, and the boss thought she stole the money."

"Oh, no!" exclaimed the second girl. "Sherry might be slow, but she wouldn't steal as much as a cookie. And she needed that job so she could buy clothes for school."

"What's so big about that?" asked another. "Don't we all need clothes?"

The second girl cut in, "If we can't earn the money, our dads buy our clothes. Sherry's dad is dead."

In the silence that followed, Joel walked away feeling miserable. He had caused that girl to lose her job. And she probably couldn't find another. Now that he knew her name, it seemed worse than ever. He hated that five dollar bill. Suddenly he squared his shoulders and went to look for Brad.

"Hey, Man!" Brad shouted. "Let's go buy that paint first thing in the morning."

"We can't," replied Joel. "I have to take that money back."

"What happened? Did you tell your folks?" asked Brad.

"No; that girl got fired for stealing."

"Maybe she gave someone else the wrong change, too."

For a minute, visions of their plane with a shiny coat of paint flashed through Joel's mind. Firmly, he pushed the thought away. "It doesn't matter," he said; "I have to give it back."

"Yeah; I guess you're right," said Brad glumly. "The Dairy Bar is still open. I'll go with you."

Joel looked at his friend gratefully. "I'll have to tell Mom where I'm going."

His mother listened carefully, a strange look on her face. Then she smiled and said, "Don't be long. And Joel—I'm glad you decided on your own to take the money back." For an instant, her hand rested lightly on his shoulder; then she gave him a little shove.

At the Dairy Bar Joel asked for the manager. A tired looking man came to the window. Joel swallowed twice, couldn't get his voice to work, and shoved the money toward him.

The man glared. "If you want to buy something, let the girl serve you. I'm trying to locate some help for tomorrow."

"That's why I'm here," Joel said as fast as he could. "Sherry wouldn't steal. She just gave me the wrong change."

The man stared at him.

Joel gulped and tried again. "I . . . I was going to keep it, and . . . and . . ." he stammered, stopped, started to turn away, then turned back. "Please, Mister," he blurted, "won't you hire her back?"

When the manager still stared, Joel mumbled, "I guess I'm the one who was stealing." Again he turned to go.

"Son!"

Joel looked back. The man still looked stunned, but he was smiling. "Thanks," he said. "I'll call Sherry right now and ask her to come back." He waved, the bill still in his hand. Joel waved back.

As the two boys started back to the picnic, Brad said, "I bet we could find some errands to run next week. And Mrs. MacIntosh's flower garden should need weeding again."

Joel stuck his hand into the pocket where the money had been. It felt cool now—and about ten pounds lighter! "Sure," he answered. "What color paint should we buy?"

Blessed are the Children

by Gloria A. Truitt

Jesus blessed the children while
    He held them on His knee,
And told the folks who gathered 'round,
    "Please, let them come to Me."

Each year, as I grow older, I
    will know He's at my side,
For I will always be His child,
    And He my constant Guide.

Other Little Ships

by Tellie Hart

The sun was sinking behind the hills as Aaron climbed up them to look down upon the shores of the Sea of Galilee.

His short legs ached. He had followed the crowds for two days, hoping to get near enough to the Healer to ask for His help. It was always the same. Someone shoved him away, blocked his way, or rudely pushed him.

Aaron shrugged. There must be thousands of people. Far below he could see the Healer sitting in a boat, pushed out into the water a little ways, too far for Aaron to hear anything. People seemed to be leaving. Perhaps now I can get through to Him, thought Aaron. He hurried back down the hill.

It was slow progress against the flow of the crowd. Everyone seemed to be in a hurry. He could hear them muttering.

"Parables! That's all He had to say today. Who wants to hear about a farmer sowing seeds? Why didn't He heal someone? That's what I came to see."

"Last week I hear He fed thousands of people. Why not today? I'm hungry. Now, everyone is ahead of us and will clean out the marketplace before we can even get there. We should have left sooner."

There were only a few people there when Aaron at last reached the lake. He turned around slowly. Where had they all gone? Where was that Healer? Perhaps He had gone to find something to eat, too. Aaron swallowed his disappointment.

Tiny waves slapped against the small boats left on shore. Farther out, large fishing boats were anchored. They all looked empty. Which one was Zebedee's? A smile played at the corner of Aaron's mouth in remembrance.

Was it only two days ago that the white-haired old man had found him hiding in the prow of the boat?

"Where did you come from, Boy?" he had demanded.

Aaron trembled, expecting a blow. He stammered. "I came from Gadara, over on the eastern shore."

"I know where Gadara is," said Zebedee angrily. "I have fished there often enough. What are you doing here in my boat? Your family must be very worried about you. How old are you, Boy?"

"I'm almost twelve," admitted Aaron quickly. "Let me work and help you on your boat. I don't have any family to worry about me . . . except, that is, for my father . . . but he's gone."

"Gone? Where? Just like those heathen there in Gadara to desert their families."

"No! He didn't desert me! He's sick."

Aaron's teeth rattled as the old man shook him. "Tell the truth, Boy" First you say your father's gone; now you say he's sick. Which is it?"

"I am telling you. My father is gone because he's sick. I've been living with my aunt; but she hates me, so I left. I want to go to the other side of the lake to find that man who heals people. Please take me with you over there. I'll work for you."

Zebedee sighed and sat down. "That would be Jesus. I've already lost two sons to Him." He paused to look keenly at the boy. "Your father, eh? Is he the one who lives in the tombs, cutting himself, running among the rocks screaming?"

Aaron nodded.

"I thought so. Your father, eh? Well, I will take you over to the other side, but don't expect too much, Boy. Jesus only works among the Jews."

Aaron scuffed his foot. "Well, why would He not heal Greeks, Romans, and everyone else?"

Zebedee did not answer. He shook his head and put his hand to the tiller.

"Now I might as well go back to Gadara," Aaron thought to himself. He was not going to be able to reach the Healer after all. It was just no use trying anymore. He would have to give up.

It was dark now on the deserted shore. Which boat out there was Zebedee's? It was hard to tell. They all looked alike in the darkness. Maybe that one over there.

Aaron fastened his sandals around his neck and swam out to the boat. No one was aboard. A night breeze sprang up as he drew himself up the anchor rope. His teeth chattered as he nestled down among some old musty rags in the bottom of the boat. Aaron pulled them over himself and fell asleep.

It was much later when he awoke with a start. The boat was moving. It was time to begin fishing. Other boats would be moving out, too. This was not Zebedee's boat. The mutter of strange voices filled him with fear.

A man's voice rose sharply. "Look at those waves! It's really starting to blow now!"

Aaron felt the spray as the boat rocked. He sneezed as water poured over him.

A man shouted. "It's a boy! What the . . . "

There was turmoil as the boat rose on a wave, then slammed down swiftly. Wind howled and shrieked. Lightning swept across the sky. Water poured into the boat with every wave that hit. Again the bow lifted and slammed down.

Aaron felt a bucket shoved into his hand.

"Bail, Boy!" someone shouted into his ear. "Bail, or we will all sink and die."

Aaron quickly obeyed. Swish, scrape, lift, throw . . . all the while holding onto the side of the boat as it lurched and pounded.

Suddenly it was over. There was an eerie calm as water slapped gently against the side of the boat. Waves stilled to a few small swells. Clouds in the sky parted to show the stars overhead. Aaron shivered with cold and fear.

"Keep bailing, Boy," ordered one of the men. "Still plenty of water left in here."

The other man spoke in the darkness. His voice was awestruck. "Did you ever see anything like this? One minute I think we are sinking; the next minute it's calm. What happened?"

"No, I never saw it like this, but it might start up again. Keep bailing, Boy!"

In the excitement, neither of the men thought to ask questions, so Aaron kept bailing. His arms ached, but he kept on until most of the water was out of the boat. Then he fell into a sound sleep.

The sun was shining when he awoke. He was alone, the boat gently rocking at anchor. Aaron drew himself up to look. Where were the men from last night?

Those cliffs! Those rocks along shore! This could only be the shoreline of Gadara! He was back home, on the eastern shore of the Sea of Galilee.

Aaron quickly dove into the water and swam to shore. As two men came over a hill, Aaron went to meet them.

"Well," grinned one of them. "Look who's up! Hey, Kid, you missed all the excitement!"

"What excitement? I thought the storm was over."

"Not the storm, Boy," corrected the other man. "It was that man called Jesus. His men say He was the one who stopped the storm last night. They said He just stood up and told it to stop! Ever hear of anything like that? I find it hard to believe."

The other man frowned. "Well, I don't know. There was something odd about the wind stopping so suddenly, right in the middle of a storm. You saw Him cure that wild man just now."

A lump rose in Aaron's throat. "What wild man?"

"Hey, Kid, you should have seen it," put in the other man, his eyes bright. "Why, that man came running and screaming, his eyes wide, his beard all matted with spittle. He was raving, I tell you. Then he just fell to the ground in front of Jesus. I couldn't hear what Jesus said, but suddenly . . . " he snapped his fingers, ". . . I tell you, I never saw anything . . . "

Aaron grabbed his tunic. "Where? Where is he?"

The man turned. "Why, right over that hill. Hey, wait,Kid . . . "

Aaron did not hear. He was running toward the hill. At the top he found several people standing in a group, talking among themselves. Aaron rushed to them.

"Where are they?" he gasped for air. "Where did they go?"

An old man looked down at him and frowned. "I don't know, Son. I heard that wild man invite them all to his house. Perhaps they went there. Did you see it, Boy? Wasn't that something!"

Aaron didn't answer. He was running again. Home! That's where they were!

Sweat poured from him as Aaron reached his home. It had been neglected so long the garden was choked with weeds; the gate had fallen off. A crowd filled the yard.

Aaron rudely shoved someone aside to get into the house. He stared, transfixed, when he saw his father. He was dressed, his face clean, his beard freshly oiled, and was sitting calmly at the feet of another man. That would be Jesus, Aaron decided.

"I appreciate your desire to come and follow Me," Jesus was saying. "Yet, sometimes it is better to stay where you are and tell others what great things God has done for you. It is best to stay where you are needed the most."

For a long moment there was silence, then Jesus looked up to meet Aaron's eyes. He glanced down at the man at his feet, then pointed to Aaron.

"There, Friend, is one who needs you most."

The Ears of Andy Spandy

by Frances Carfi Matranga

Andy Spandy was eight years old and had red hair and freckles. He lived in a cottage with his mother, who was a widow. He had a sweet, friendly smile. He also had ears that stuck out from his head like the handles on a loving cup. Not even long hair could hide those ears.

Poor Andy. More than anything he wanted to look like the other children. Oh, to have ears that lay flat against his head instead of a pair that stuck out like wings!

The boys and girls on his block made fun of Andy— especially Dennis. "Hey, Dumbo, have you tried flying?" he would tease. "Wiggle your ears and I bet you'll take off." And then he'd laugh.

Sometimes when Andy went to the park the children made a circle around him and chanted:

> "Big Ears, Big Ears,
> Oh, what a funny sight!
> Someday, someday,
> Andy will soar like a kite!"

They sang it over and over again until tears glistened in Andy's eyes. Once he shouted, "My ears won't always be like this! My mother is saving up to have a doctor fix them."

The children thought he was making that up . . . and so they teased him even more. When this happened Andy would run home, vowing never to go back to the park. Yet he always went back. He liked wading in the brook and swinging on the swings and climbing the monkey bars.

When nobody else was there he would take off his shirt and pretend he was a *torero*, a bullfighter . . . like the ones he had seen in a film on television. He pretended his shirt was a red cape and he'd wave it at an imaginary bull, calling, *"Toro! Eh, toro!"* Then he'd stand his ground while the huge black beast came charging toward him. At the last moment, with a swing of the cape, he would maneuver the bull past him without shifting his feet, like the bravest of *toreros*.

When the neighborhood children played tag or dodge ball in the park, Andy would sit under a tree and watch. Always he hoped they would invite him to join them. But they never did. He was very lonely.

Sometimes Andy hated the boys and girls for not liking him. But he couldn't hate them for long. It was wrong to hate. He had learned that in Sunday school. And he tried to forgive as Jesus does; but, oh . . . sometimes it was hard to do.

What could he do to make the neighborhood kids stop teasing him, he wondered.

In school it wasn't too bad. Nobody made fun of him in front of his teacher. Her name was Mrs. Benson. Andy liked her. He paid close attention to the lessons and was the best student in his third-grade class. He might be funny-looking, but nobody was going to call Andy Spandy stupid. No sir!

One Friday evening, Andy saw his mother sew a snap on her blouse. It gave him an interesting idea. Wouldn't it be terrific if he could snap his ears flat to his head!

Of course, you couldn't sew the snaps on your ears. But maybe there was some other way. Andy put on his thinking cap.

> He thought . . .
> And he thought . . .
> And he thought . . .

And then . . . hey! What an idea!

"Mom," he said, trying to hide his excitement because he didn't know if it would work, "do me a favor, will you? Sew two snaps to four short strips of adhesive tape."

"Oh? What for?" she wanted to know.

"I just want to try something," he said. "If it works, I'll show you."

"Big snaps or little snaps?"

"Big. They've got to be strong," he said.

Twenty minutes later, Andy was in the bathroom in front of the mirror. Very carefully he stuck two of the adhesive strips onto the back of his ears. The other two strips he stuck to the sides of his head behind his ears. Then he pressed down hard on the ears with his thumbs. Ouch!

The snaps snapped together. But would they hold?

They did! And his ears looked great! They looked like anybody's else's ears. Only a *little* big. It seemed too good to be true.

"Oh, boy!" Andy shouted gleefully and ran to show his mother.

Mrs. Spandy was astonished . . . and very impressed. She thought it clever of him to come up with such an original idea. Andy's longish hair now covered the back of his ears and concealed the snaps and tapes.

Andy decided to stay indoors that weekend so that none of the kids would see him. Then, when he appeared in school on Monday, they would think he'd been away to get his ears fixed.

On Monday morning, when Andy walked into class, his stomach churned as though it had a pinwheel inside.

All eyes turned in his direction.

Silence fell over the room like a blanket. Everyone gawked at him.

Then a little blond girl named Susie said, "He wasn't kidding about getting his ears fixed!"

The children began crowding around Andy, all talking at once.

"Neat, man!"

"You look great, Andy."

"I never woulda believed it!"

"Did the doctor use stitches? Can I see them?" one boy asked, lifting a lock of Andy's hair. "Oh, there's tape over the stitches."

"Don't touch." Andy pulled away quickly.

"There's the bell, children," Mrs. Benson spoke up. "Take your seats, please."

Andy sat down with a sigh of relief. The pinwheel in his stomach had stopped turning. Everything was going to be okay.

The next two days were good days for Andy. The children treated him like anybody else. They played with him in the park after school. He was one of them at last. How good it felt not to be laughed at, not to be lonely!

But then on Wednesday something awful happened. Mrs. Benson had asked Andy to erase the blackboard. And there, in full view of the whole class, one of his ears suddenly popped out. The tape was losing its sticking power. One ear was flat and the other stuck out like a wing.

The next minute the whole classroom was in an uproar. The children shrieked with laughter. Even Mrs. Benson couldn't stop them.

Poor Andy. Tears flooded his eyes as he clapped a hand over the offending ear and dashed out of the room. Everybody would soon know what had happened. The whole school would be laughing at him.

He ran all the way home, choking back sobs. He ran to his room and threw himself on the bed. All the hurt spilled out and he cried and cried until his tears were all used up.

Exhausted, he whispered, "Please, God, make them stop laughing at me."

He sighed and closed his eyes and fell asleep.

The next day the two third grades took a field trip. Mrs. Benson and Miss Lewis had arranged to take their pupils to a large dairy farm and milk-processing plant some miles out of town. The children enjoyed the bus ride and chattered all the way. Wearing his favorite red shirt, Andy sat next to Mrs. Benson. He watched out the window the whole trip and did not talk to anyone.

At the dairy farm, the children learned how the milking was done with electric milkers. Fifty cows at a time stood on a circular, revolving table where they were washed, dried, and milked, all within 12½ minutes.

One of the dairy workers showed the children the machines that separated the cream from the milk. Other machines pasteurized, cooled, and bottled it. The whole process took only minutes. Andy found it very interesting.

The teachers and children had brought their lunches to eat at the dairy farm. The teachers ate at a picnic table beneath one of the maple trees. The children spread out on the grass.

Close by, a stone wall surrounded a meadow. In it stood a black bull with long, sharp horns. When the children called to him, the bull tossed his head and ran through red poppies and other wild flowers to the far side of the meadow. There he lay down with his back to them, as though he didn't want to be bothered.

After lunch, the children had a lesson under the tree about the dairy farm. The teachers asked questions as to what they had learned. Andy knew every answer that the others missed. He even remembered the name of the circular, revolving table on which the cows were milked: *rotolactor*. But the sad feeling was still inside him. It was almost like an ache. Even though there were some 50 children around him, he felt alone.

Lapsing into a daydream, he thought, *Maybe I'll be president of the United States when I grow up. Then they'll be sorry they laughed at me. They'll want to come and see me at the White House, but maybe I won't want to see them. My ears will be fixed by then and I'll have lots of new friends. Sure. But . . . why can't these kids be my friends? right now? just as I am? I hate these ears. I hate them!*

Suddenly one of the children pointed toward the bull's meadow. "Look!"

There was Susie in the meadow. She had disobeyed orders—she had sneaked away from the group in order to pick wild flowers in the meadow. The bull was still reclining at the far end, with his back to her. Thinking he was asleep, she had wandered almost to the center of the field where red poppies grew in a thick cluster.

"Susie!" cried Mrs. Benson, jumping up. "Susie, come back here!"

At that moment the bull rose to his feet, turned, and saw the little girl. He began snorting angrily. It was as if he was saying, "This is *my* field!"

"Susie, look out!" the children shouted as the bull began running toward her. They were all on their feet now, scared.

Susie screamed and dropped her bouquet. She turned to run, but in her excitement she tripped over her own feet and fell to her knees.

Meanwhile, Andy had pulled off his shirt and was climbing the field-stone wall. He knew how deadly the horns of a bull could be. He had seen them gore a horse in the bullfighting film.

There was only one thing to do—distract the bull's attention away from Susie so she'd have a chance to make it to safety. There was no time to think twice. There wasn't even time to be afraid. Andy simply did what he knew had to be done.

40

Leaping into the meadow, he ran toward the bull, waving his shirt to attract its attention.

Susie was up and running now.

"Toro! Eh, toro!" Andy shouted, fluttering his shirt with both hands. "Here, *toro*, here!"

It worked! Seeing the shirt waving like a flag, the *toro* swerved to attack it.

"Oh, God, give wings to my feet now," Andy prayed, his heart pounding. Whirling, he fled for his life.

Never had he run so fast!

He made it just in time, scrambling over the wall with the speed of a lizard, banging a knee in the process. No sooner had he dropped to the ground, than he heard a horn scraping rock. The bull had swerved at the last moment to keep from crashing headlong into the wall.

Andy sat on the ground, panting, his arms hugging the bruised knee. Now that the danger was past, he began to shake. The others came rushing over to him, cheering his bravery. Some of the girls were crying.

"Man, did you fly," Dennis exclaimed, reaching out a hand to help Andy up. "I never knew you could run so fast."

"Me neither," Andy admitted with a breathless little laugh. In his mind he prayed, *Thank you, God, for putting wings on my feet.*

"I'm sorry, Mrs. Benson, I'm sorry," Susie sobbed. "I'll never do anything like that again." She grabbed Andy's hand and squeezed it. "Thank you, Andy, for saving me."

The teachers hugged him with tears in their eyes.

"That was very brave of you, Andy," Mrs. Benson said, her voice all quivery. "But you took an awful chance. How did you know what to do?"

"I saw it in a bullfight movie on TV," he said shyly. "That's what Spanish *toreros* do—they wave capes to get the bull's attention. I thought if I could do it, it would give Susie time to get away."

"Oh, Andy, suppose you hadn't watched that movie!" said Susie. Her eyes widened. "Do you suppose . . . God had something to do with your watching it? I'd be dead now if it weren't for you!" She began to cry again. "I'm sorry I made fun of your ears. Never again!"

Dennis shuffled his feet, looking uncomfortable. "That goes for me, too," he said huskily.

"Me, too. Sorry, Andy," other voices chimed in.

Andy took a deep breath and smiled his sweet, friendly smile. The ache inside him was beginning to go away. And to think he almost hadn't come today.

"I think you all realize now that Andy has a loving heart," said Mrs. Benson. "He risked his life to save Susie. He would have done the same for any one of you, I'm sure." She looked around at all the children. "So tell me, what does the size of ears or nose or anything else matter when the heart is so big and brave and generous? That's what God looks at, you know—our hearts."

There was a long pause.

Then Dennis grinned and punched Andy playfully on the arm. "Hey, *torero*, how about sitting next to me on the way home. I wanna hear about that bullfight movie."

"Sure," said Andy, grinning back. "Why not?"

Heaven

by Nathanael Lloyd

Behold! God's emerald-rainbowed throne:
A city as precious as jasper stone;
Christ's glorious, lofty, and holy chair;
How golden the bowls bearing fragrant prayer;
The life-giving river, that crystal stream,
More beauteous than any believer's dream;
The garments of white and the crowns of gold
Shine bright as a light from the men of old
Composing on harps made of gold, ablaze,
With thousands of palm branches waving in praise.

God's glorious mansion, unbounded rooms,
Prepared for His bride by dear Jesus, our Groom.
Behold the foundation, the twelve firm gates,
A radiant angel at each one waits;
Foundations bejeweled with gems unblurred—
Yellow and quick as the hummingbird,
Orange as the lily, and purplish as wine,
Waxen and green as the olive vine,
Ruddy red ruby, and bold richest blue—
Through which the magnificent Light shines true.
Each of the gates of a single pearl,
Where praises, the banners of God, unfurl.
A city of gold, and as clear as glass,
Where last are the first, and the first are last.

Daystar and moon won't display their face
In heavenly home. No sinful trace
Shadows the glory of Jesus' grace.
Here is our rest, God's holiest place.

Clouds

by Reta Spears

Tania and Willa Jo giggled so hard at the cloud shapes that Tania got the hiccups. Just as they were stopping, Willa Jo squealed again. "Look! Look! It's a cat with a pickle on its head!" she cried. Both girls held their sides and laughed until Willa Jo rolled off the bed. After a while they caught their breath.

Tania and Willa Jo looked out the window again at the moonlit clouds. The girls were pretending the clouds were whatever the shapes brought to mind. So far they had seen a horse riding a potato, a fish with an umbrella, and a ballerina with two tutus.

"I love it when you can stay overnight," exclaimed Tania. "Maybe we'll laugh all night!"

"Not if your mom hears us," said Willa Jo. "Hey! Look at that one! It's Jerky James," she began to hoot with laughter.

Tania laughed too, but her heart wasn't in it. James couldn't help his jerky movements, she knew. Yet, most of the kids in their third-grade room called him that when he wasn't around.

"Willa Jo," said Tania, her laughter gone for the moment, "maybe we shouldn't call him 'Jerky' James."

"Why not? Everyone calls him that. He doesn't know the difference."

"Well, it's not very nice."

"Oh, brother! You're such a baby!"

"I am not," protested Tania and gave her friend a gentle push on the shoulder.

"You are!" said Willa Jo and tumbled Tania off the bed.

"Oof!" said Tania and rubbed her bumped knee. "You're the jerky one, Willa Jo!" she declared. She grabbed a pillow with both hands and lifted it high in the air. "Floop!" She brought it down on Willa Jo's head.

"Hey!" cried Willa Jo, and a second pillow swept through the air. Tania felt it whump against her stomach. She sat down unexpectedly on the floor. A handful of feathers escaped from the pillow seam and floated upward. One perched on Tania's nose. The sight of it started Willa Jo laughing again. Tania meant to stay angry, but the feather tickled, and she knew it must look funny. So the two of them howled in glee.

A half-expected voice called from downstairs. "Tania!"

The laughter came to a sudden stop. "Yes, Mother?"

"That's enough noise, now. Quiet down, or I'll have to separate you two."

"Okay, Mom."

Willa Jo sat very straight and folded her hands on her lap. She held her lips in a tight line, slightly curved up at the corners. He eyes looked up in an angelic pose. Tania smothered a giggle with both hands.

Suddenly Willa Jo said, "Tania, do you love Jerk . . . I mean, James?"

Tania started to blurt no, but something made her stop. "I don't know," she answered. "I know we're supposed to."

"What d'you mean?" asked Willa Jo.

"Well, I know Jesus loves James the same as He loves us—so maybe we could try."

"Yeah," agreed Willa Jo, "but how can you love someone you don't really know? And how can you get to know them when they're so different from everybody else?"

"Maybe he's not so different," said Tania.

"Huh!" snorted Willa Jo. "Why do you think they call him 'Jerky'? James can't even walk right. And he talks jerky, besides. You can't get much different-er."

45

"But maybe he's the same inside," said Tania. "Maybe he's just like you and me and needs some friends."

"S'pose he does," said Willa Jo cautiously. "But friends of his might get laughed at like he does. Who'd like that?"

"We might."

"What?"

"We wouldn't like being laughed at, but we might like being friends with James," said Tania. Something she remembered made her feel excited. "You know some of those 'friends' verses we learned in Sunday school?" She recited, "Do not forsake your friend."

"Yeah," remembered Willa Jo. "A friend loves at all times," she quoted. Then she said in excitement, "I just thought of something! Maybe James is kind-a like that guy we learned about in the Bible last Sunday. You know, the poor guy all ragged and funny looking. They made him sit on a little stool all by himself just because of how he looked."

"Yeah!" exclaimed Tania. "And that was from the book of James."

Both girls grew silent and looked out the window for a while.

"What'll we say to James?" asked Willa Jo.

Tania replied, "We could tell him about the clouds."

Grandma's Grandma's Quilt

by Louise Ulmer

When Todd's grandmother gave him a quilt made by her grandmother, his mother was overjoyed. She loved antiques, but Todd couldn't see what all the fuss was about. His mother even wanted to hang the quilt on the wall. Todd thought that was dumb.

That night, as a cold breeze rattled the trees, Todd got up to close his window. In the corner he saw Grandma's quilt, folded neatly on a chair. Todd spread the blanket on his bed and crawled under it. The quilt was soft and warm.

When Todd awoke the next morning, he sat up and looked at the quilt on his bed. It was full of squares, and each square showed a different picture. The first square was a ship with giant white sails. Next to it was a log church, and next to that a log fort. There were pictures of people at Christmas and the Fourth of July.

When his mother came in to wake him, Todd asked about the pictures. Mother explained, "Your grandma's grandma couldn't read or write. She never had time to go to school. In those days, girls were not expected to learn from books; there was too much work to do at home. Women had to make everything their family used. They even had to spin the cotton and wool to make thread for clothing and bedding. Anyway, your grandma's grandma—her name was Gretchen—couldn't write, but she could draw pictures. One day she decided to tell the story of her life. Since she couldn't write, she made this quilt. The ship is a picture of the one that brought Gretchen and her family to this country from Europe."

"I see," said Todd. "It's like a picture album."

"Exactly," Mother said. "That's why we call it an Album Quilt."

"What about this church?" asked Todd.

"The church is the first building the family built in the new land. All the immigrants on the ship belonged to the same church, and they brought their old world faith with them to their new home. When they arrived, they went right to work building a church first. They wanted God to have the best house in town. They knew if they put God first, everything else in their lives would be all right."

"Then they built the town, right?" asked Todd, pointing to the houses inside the big fort.

"That's right," said Mother. Then she pointed to another picture square. "Can you tell what this one is all about?"

Todd recognized it immediately. "That's the inside of our church. There's the cross and the altar and the symbols of the Apostles."

"Yes. This is the place where all Gretchen's children were baptized and married."

"There's Christmas dinner," Todd said, smoothing a square on the corner. "And here's Thanksgiving."

"Right," Mother said. "Grandma Gretchen put in every important event of her life. She also sewed the pictures in the quilt from scraps of clothing her family had worn. There are pieces of Grandpa's shirts, Grandma's dresses, and over there—scraps of my baby dresses."

"Please don't take the quilt off my bed yet," said Todd. "I want to study it for a while each night before I go to bed."

"I think that's exactly what Grandma Gretchen hoped you would do," said Mother.

That night Todd went to sleep thinking about Grandma's Grandma Gretchen. It was nice to know that he was part of her story, sharing the same faith in the same Father, Son, and Holy Spirit, worshiping in the same church and learning about the same apostles. Someday, he decided, he would share the story of Grandma's Grandma's faith—his faith, too.

A Shot for Margaret

by Muriel Steffy Lipp

Margaret stormed into the room, banged her books down on the living room table, kicked off her shoes, and said, "This is one awful day!"

"Why, Margaret—what's wrong?" asked Mother.

"I have to get a shot," said Margaret, waving a form for parents to take to the county health center. "Please, Mom! Say I don't have to get it. I hate shots! Please, Mom?" Margaret's pleading eyes searched her mother's.

Mother read the form. "It's for German measles. Don't know how we missed getting it earlier. You need to get the shot now so you won't get the disease as an adult. It's more serious then."

"Oh, Mom—I don't care about when I'm an adult. Please don't make me."

"You don't care now, but you'd care very much then. As your mom, I want to take care of the whole Margaret, not just the now Margaret."

The now Margaret, tears oozing from her eyes, ran to her room and shut the door.

Her little sister, Louise, who shared her room, said, "Don't worry, Margaret. It won't hurt much. Let's play doctor." So, Margaret and Louise gave shots to each other with toy syringes.

Later in the afternoon, Louise came to Mother with a worried look. "Mom, Margaret is burying money in the ground. She shouldn't do that, should she?"

"Don't worry about it, Louise. I'll talk to Margaret later."

That night, when Mother was saying good night to Margaret, she asked, "Margaret, Louise told me you were burying some money. Do you want to tell me about it?"

50

"I guess so. It was a dime and a nickle. My own money! I buried them to give to God. Maybe God can save me from the shot."

"Margaret, you don't have to pay God to help you."

"Well, I thought if I gave God some money . . . you know . . . it just might help God to remember me."

"But, Margaret, suppose God cares for the whole Margaret as I do. And, suppose God thinks of the shot as a good thing."

"Well, we'll see."

Mother kissed Margaret, then prayed, "God, Your will be done with Margaret. Let her know that You love her and will stay by her side—even during hard times. In Jesus' name. Amen."

"What does 'Your will be done' mean?" asked Margaret.

"You know, it's in the Lord's Prayer. It means, do to Margaret what You want, not just what she wants."

"I don't like that prayer," said Margaret.

"It's a hard prayer," agreed Mother. "But, God never promised to save us from things, just to be with us."

"You mean, God isn't going to come through?"

"God will come through, but maybe not in the way you want."

After breakfast on shot day, Mother said, "Let's go to the clinic."

Margaret looked sad. "It looks as though God forgot me."

"Wait and see," said Mother.

At the clinic they took seats in the waiting room. Margaret was afraid. She felt a heaviness in her stomach. She was scared of shots—more than of getting a tooth filled or of taking bad-tasting medications.

Several other parents and kids were sitting in the waiting room. One girl smiled shyly at Margaret.

"Sally," said Margaret, "what are you doing here?" Sally was in Margaret's class in school.

"I have to get a shot," said Sally.

"Me too," said Margaret.

Sally looked even more scared than Margaret. She was twisting the end of her sweater very tight. When the nurse called her name, Sally clung to her mother.

Margaret felt sorry for her and, before she knew what she was doing, Margaret offered to go first.

"Well, okay," said Sally.

"I'm just as scared as you are, Sally. But Mom said it won't hurt much. It's fast."

Margaret marched into the shot room, rolling up her sleeve. Her heart was ka-bumping, but she felt very brave. Helping Sally somehow helped Margaret. Was that what Mom meant about Jesus being with her, Margaret wondered.

The nurse rubbed Margaret's arm with alcohol, and Margaret breathed deeply and closed her eyes. She prayed, "God, I'm scared." Then she could feel the needle prick her arm. In a flash it was out. As Margaret opened her eyes, she could see the nurse pressing a pad with alcohol against her arm. It was over. "Thank You, Jesus."

Margaret marched triumphantly out to the waiting room. She noticed Sally's scared eyes following her.

"It doesn't hurt much, Sally. Honest. Just close your eyes. If I can do it, you can."

After they got home, Margaret said to her mother, "I guess God did help me with that shot. And I helped Sally. She was more scared than I was."

"You're right," said Mom. "Just one thing, Margaret. That fifteen cents you buried—why not dig it up and give it to help people who don't have enough food to eat?"

"Okay," said Margaret, skipping off in search for a shovel.

Made that Way

by Diane Christian Boehm

There was one thing everybody knew about Joel: He hated to go to bed. He considered sleeping a waste of time. He was sure something wonderful would happen while he was sleeping, and he didn't want to miss it.

Joel had more ways to avoid going to bed than anyone. He knew all the usual tricks, like having to go to the bathroom again, or needing a drink of water, or begging for an extra story or hug. Sometimes he would creep out of bed and sit on the stairs to hear what was going on. One time he fell asleep there and tumbled all the way down and landed on his head.

He knew other tricks, too. One time he pretended a loose tooth had come out and had gotten lost in the bed, so he took all the sheets and blankets off his bed. Once he even crawled into a corner of the downstairs closet and hid, making his mother so angry and worried that he was grounded for two days. But even that didn't stop his tricks. He went on, doing just about anything he could think of to avoid going to bed.

It didn't matter to him at all that some mornings he felt very tired and cranky. Once in a while he even missed the school bus because he was too tired to remember where he had left his shoes. And sometimes he would put his head down during class, fall asleep, miss the assignment for the next day, and not do the homework. Then he would get his name on the board, and his teacher would send a note home to his parents.

One weekend he was invited to stay with his Uncle John. Joel was very happy, for Uncle John was one of his favorite people. Uncle John always got a pizza for them

53

to share or took him out for an ice cream sundae. Because Uncle John worked at a zoo, he had lots of interesting books and pictures of animals. He could tell lots of stories about the people who came to see the animals. Best of all, Joel was *sure* Uncle John would not make him go to bed if he didn't want to.

But, when it was bedtime, Uncle John said the same thing his mother always said. "Time for bed, Joel."

"Why do I have to go to bed? I'm not tired," Joel pleaded. "I hate to go to bed! Please, will you tell me another story?"

Uncle John thought for a while. "All right," he agreed; "I'll tell you why we have bedtime. But when I'm finished, you must go right to bed with no more argument. Agreed?"

"Oh, all right." Joel didn't like the agreement, but he did want to hear Uncle John's story.

Uncle John began. "Long ago, when God made the world, He gave it an orderly way to run. Each day has 24 hours. Each day has a sunrise, a daytime, and a sunset followed by a night. God designed it that way. He created the sun to give light to the earth. Because our earth is a huge ball, the light of the sun shines on only half of it at a time. That half where the sun is shining is day; the other half is night."

"Are we on the day side or the night side?" Joel wanted to know.

"Both. The earth turns completely around once every day. You can't feel it, but it's happening. When our part of the earth turns toward the sun, we see the sunrise. The sun shines brightest in the middle of the day. Then, when our side turns away from the sun, we get sunset. Night comes when our half of the earth turns completely away from the sun's light.

"God made day and night because He knew that His creatures needed time to work and time to rest. For most people, daytime is their time to work and be busy, and nighttime is their peaceful, quiet time to rest. Plants, animals and people all need time for work and for rest."

"I'd rather use all my time to play," Joel spoke up. "Resting is a waste of time."

"Not so. Resting is very important for our bodies. When we rest, our bodies are renewed. Our bodies grow and they get the strength to fight off germs and sickness. Even our brains need to rest. God made us that way. With good sleep each night, we take care of our bodies, we feel happier, and we can work or play at our best the next day. That's how God made us, and that's why we have bedtime. So—good night. See you in the morning." Uncle John turned out the light and left the room.

The next day, Joel woke up very excited. Uncle John had promised to take him to the zoo where he worked.

The day was wonderful! Uncle John showed Joel lots of special places that most zoo visitors never get to see. He saw some baby birds pecking their way out of their shells. He visited the infirmary, the zoo hospital for sick animals. He visited the kitchens where the food for all the many types of animals was weighed or measured out. There were fish counted out in buckets for the penguins; lettuce, orange slices and chunks of fruit for the monkeys; large hunks of meat for the panthers. Each animal received the diet it needed to be healthy and strong.

That night Joel was full of the adventures of the day. He was sure he didn't need to go to bed—not now when he and Uncle John could go on talking about everything they had seen that day!

Finally Uncle John sighed. "You may not want to go to bed," he yawned, "but I sure do. It's been a very busy day, and my body needs the rest. Remember what I told you last night?"

But Joel had made up his mind. He was not going to let himself be talked into going to bed this time. "I'll bet giraffes never have to go to bed," he said. "I've never seen a giraffe sleep."

"Oh, yes, they do," Uncle John answered. "In fact, just as every creature looks different, eats different foods, lives in its own way and has its own special place in the world, so each one has its own way to rest. Let me tell you about giraffes. They run very fast to escape enemies, or use their strong necks to hit them. But, when they sit down to rest, they curve their necks backwards and rest their head on their back hip. Since it's risky to sleep in this position, giraffes sleep only about ten minutes at a time."

"Well, isn't there any animal that never sleeps? If I can think of an animal that doesn't sleep, then will you let me stay up as long as I want?"

Uncle John smiled, for he already knew the answer. But he also knew that Joel would never be satisfied until he tried to find an animal that doesn't need sleep.

"How about bats?" Joel was sure he'd come up with the perfect answer. "They fly around all night long, don't they? They don't sleep."

"But they do, Joel. Bats and many other animals are nocturnal. That means they rest during the day and are active at night, the best time to catch the insects and other small animals they eat.

"Bats sleep most of the day—upside down. They sleep in a large group with other bats, often hanging by only one foot, with their wings folded around their bodies.

"Bats don't need light to see because they use sound waves like radar; the high-pitched sound they make bounces off other objects and back to their ears, telling them where the objects are so they can avoid flying into them. Even with hundreds of bats in the same cave, they hardly ever fly into each other. So, you see, Joel, bats do sleep; they just sleep in a way different from people—a way suited to the way God made them."

Joel thought for a minute. "I know! I'll bet seals don't have to sleep. How could they? They live in the water."

"God made seals in a special way, too. They take short naps just below the surface of the water. When they go under, they close their noses and ears to keep out the water. When their brain signals a need for more oxygen, they float to the surface, breathe, and then sink slowly beneath the surface again, still sound asleep. God has given them this unusual way to sleep, perfectly suited to the way they live."

This was getting harder than Joel had thought it would be. He thought for a long time. Uncle John yawned again. "What about bears?" Joel spoke quickly. "I didn't see any bears sleeping at the zoo today."

"Let me tell you about bears," said Uncle John. "Bears, raccoons and many other animals sleep all winter. They hibernate. They eat a lot of food all summer to build up a layer of fat under their skin. Then, when winter comes, they find a cave or hollow tree in which to sleep. While they are hibernating, their breathing slows down to save energy, and they live off their fat deposits. Some hibernating animals do not even eat or drink for four or five months until they awaken again in the spring."

"Four or five months?" Joel couldn't imagine anything sleeping that long! He could see he was getting nowhere. He gave one last try. "What about the king of beasts, the lion? He's so strong, I'll bet he doesn't have to sleep at all if he doesn't want to."

"Remember all those people at the lion's cave today, waiting and waiting for him to come out—but he never did? Do you know what he was doing? He had just been fed, so he may not come out for two whole days because he is sleeping all that time. Lions, especially those living in the wild, gorge and rest. They eat as much food as they can hold, sometimes up to 50 pounds. Then they rest for up to two days while their body digests the huge meal they have devoured."

Joel could not think of any more animals to name. He was even starting to feel a little bit sleepy. Suddenly he yawned a big yawn. "I guess you win," he was forced to admit, with a little smile on his face. "If God made every other creature to need rest, maybe He made me that way, too." He tried not to yawn again. "I guess I'll go to bed now."

And, he did.

Moon Tale

by Louise Ulmer

Nada and Diep sat on the fire escape outside the window of the tenth-floor apartment where Nada lived. "Diep," she asked, "where do you think the sun goes at night?"

Diep answered, "The sun goes to California and then goes to shine on my family in Vietnam."

"How do you know that?" Nada asked.

"When I was a little girl in Vietnam, I went to a Christian school. My teacher told me that when the sun shines on Vietnam, it is dark in the United States. Now I am in the United States, so it must be the other way around."

This night, the moon rose red and glowing, like fire. "Diep," asked Nada, "what's wrong with the moon? It looks more like the sun."

"In my country we have a story about the red moon," said Diep. "Some people believe the moon is the foolish warlord, Tham Lam, whose name means 'greedy.' Tham Lam went throughout the countryside cheating poor peasants out of their rice farms and eating all their rice. He got so fat he could no longer see his arms and legs. He was round as a ball. When the great King of the East called him to account for his deeds, Tham Lam could no longer walk, but had to roll to the palace. For punishment, the king told Tham Lam that he must work for all eternity to make up for his crimes. Forever he would have to roll around on the outside of heaven and shine brightly so the peasants could have light to see by when it was dark, and have something pretty to look at when their work was done."

"I like that story," said Nada. "I think I know why the moon is red or gold and not always white."

"What is the answer?" asked Diep.

"Tham Lam likes to change shirts." Diep and Nada laughed at that.

After a few minutes of watching the moon in silence, Diep said, "When I went to Christian school, I learned another story about the moon. In the Bible it says God created the sun and moon and stars on the fourth day of the very first week. Before that, He had created light and heaven and earth. After that, He created birds and animals and people. We were taught that our Father in heaven made all things good and beautiful for people to use and enjoy and care for. Now that I am a Christian, I know the first story is a folk tale and the Bible story is true."

Mama came to the fire escape and said, "Bedtime, girls."

"Look, Mama," Nada said, pointing to the moon. "We know why the moon is red."

"Oh, yes," said Mama. "I saw it on TV, too. The red color comes from pollution in the air around the earth's surface."

Nada and Diep looked at each other and smiled. "No, Mama," said Nada, giggling. "Stay here while we get ready for bed, and I'll tell you a moon tale."

Somebody Made the World

by Sharon Lee Roberts

Somebody made the world.
Do you know who?

Somebody made the sunny yellow daffodils
that dance in the springtime wind.
Do you know who?

Somebody made the turtles and butterflies and robins
that climb and fly and sing to me in the summertime.
Do you know who?

Somebody made the trees
    with so many autumn leaves
that I have to use every crayon in the box
when I draw a picture of them.
Do you know who?

Somebody made the gentle snowflakes
    that cover the ground
like a soft white blanket in wintertime,
Somebody who knows I like to slide down the big hill
on my red sled.
Do you know who?

Somebody made the rain
that makes me feel cozy in my warm house,
and the sun that warms me all the way through
and makes me feel happy.
Do you know who?

Somebody put the sky up there
and filled it with fluffy white clouds in the daytime,
making me think of cotton candy,

and tiny white stars at night
that twinkle like sparkles against dark blue velvet.
Do you know who?

I do.
He's Someone who made me—and you, too—
and the whole world.

God did it all.

"Thank You, God."

Vandalism!

by Frances Carfi Matranga

"Lena Brown, what were you doing in my clubhouse?" Diana shouted angrily as the girl came out the door.

Lena's face turned red. Quickly, she darted away into the woods that bordered Diana's backyard.

Diana ran to the playhouse and looked inside.

What a mess! The table and chairs were overturned. Plastic cups and saucers were scattered on the floor. The pages of a book had been torn and flung everywhere. And the sheer window curtain had a long rip in it.

Tearful and angry, Diana ran to tell her mother. Mother followed her to the playhouse to see the damage.

"That Lena Brown!" Diana fumed.

"Why would she want to do this?" Mother asked.

"Because I wouldn't let her join my club."

"Perhaps . . . ," Mother began.

"But, Mom, we already have four members. We would be too crowded with five kids in this one little room. I explained that to Lena, but she wouldn't listen. She got mad. And now this!"

"Well, it could be worse," Mother said. "I can sew the curtain. But we can't fix the book. Too bad." She lifted the little table. "Clean up the mess, Honey, then come to the house and we'll talk about it."

By the time Diana finished straightening the playhouse, she had calmed a little, but was still angry.

"I know what you're going to tell me, Mom," she said as she flopped down on the sofa. "I should love my neighbor. But Lena's my enemy now."

Mother picked up her Bible and turned to Matthew 5. "Read verse 44, Diana," she said. "It's from the Sermon on the Mount. Jesus is speaking."

Diana leaned over and read, "Love your enemies." "Oh," she said. "I forgot He said that."

"Didn't He love his enemies?" her mother reminded. "Even those who nailed Him to the cross? He died for *everybody's* sins . . . Lena's as well as yours. Jesus loves the sinner and is always ready to forgive. If He can be loving and kind to you, shouldn't you be to Lena?"

"You mean I'm supposed to be kind even to people who are mean to me?"

"Yes," Mother said, "but we have to depend on the Lord to help us. As Christians, we want to be as much like Jesus as possible, don't we?"

Diana nodded slowly.

"Lena is probably scared right now," Mother continued. "She didn't expect to be caught. She probably thinks you're going to tell her parents. How do you suppose she'd react if you went over to see her as a friend instead?"

"She'd be surprised, I guess. But I don't feel a bit friendly toward her," Diana muttered.

"I know, dear," Mother said. "You need the Lord's help for that. Why don't you pray about it?"

"Well . . . okay."

Diana's feet dragged on the way upstairs to her room. Kneeling by her bed, she prayed, "Lord, You know I don't feel like being nice to Lena. Please take away the angry feeling and help me be more like You."

She leaned her head against the mattress. As she knelt there quietly, she pictured Jesus nailed to the cross. *Father, forgive them, for they know not what they do.*

Diana could almost hear Jesus saying the words. A lump rose in her throat. How could He be so kind and loving even while bleeding and hurting so?

She began to think about Lena. Her family did not go to church. Lena did not go to Sunday school. Perhaps she should invite her.

Diana jumped up and ran downstairs. "I'm going over to see Lena now," she told her mother.

Mother smiled and nodded.

Diana ran the two blocks to Lena's house. Lena answered her knock.

"I knew you'd come," she said curtly. "Well, nobody's home but me." She started to shut the door.

"I just wanted you to know I'm not mad at you," Diana said quickly.

"You're not?" Lena opened the door wider. "Then you're not going to tell my parents?"

"No. Don't worry," Diana assured her. "Listen, Lena, would you like to have lemonade and homemade cookies with me in the clubhouse?"

Lena stared at her. "After what I did? W-Why would you want me?" she stammered.

"Jesus wants me to forgive." Diana offered her hand. "Shake?"

Lena swallowed. Her eyes grew moist. "Thanks, Diana," she said as she gripped her hand. "I'm sorry for what I did. You're . . . well, you're super."

"Am I? It must be because of the Lord, Lena. He helps me to love people. I was angry at you, but He helped me get over it."

"He helped you?" Lena looked puzzled but interested. "How? He's far away."

"Let's go to the playhouse and talk about it while we have our lemonade and cookies, okay?" Diana suggested.

"Okay." Lena was smiling now. "You're somethin' else. You really are!"

Diana felt good inside as they walked together. Jesus had helped her make a friend out of an enemy.

How Did God Get to Arkansas?

by Elaine Watson

Jondavid and his little sister, Andrea, were getting ready for bed in their new house in their new town in Arkansas. They had just moved to Arkansas with their mother and father. They were very tired after the long ride from Delaware.

"Why did we move to Arkansas?" Jondavid asked his mother.

"Because Daddy has a new job and a new office," she told him.

"We're a long way from Delaware, aren't we?" Jondavid said. "We didn't forget my swing, did we?"

"We brought your swing," said his mother as she brushed Andrea's hair. "And soon you will have lots of new friends here."

Jondavid yawned.

"Time for bed," said his mother. "Who wants to pray first?"

"I do," said Andrea. She bowed her head and closed her eyes. Suddenly she looked up at her mother. "Can God hear me pray in Arkansas?"

Jondavid blurted to his sister, "God lives in Delaware. He's far away at our old house and our old church."

Their mother smiled. "God lives in Arkansas, too. He can hear your prayers here in our new house just as He did in our old house in Delaware."

Andrea was puzzled. "How did God get to Arkansas?"

"Did He come in a car?" asked Jondavid.

"I think He came in an airplane," said Andrea.

"Let's go ask Daddy," said Jondavid as he jumped out of bed.

Andrea and Jondavid found their daddy in the living room, unpacking some books and putting them on a shelf.

"How did God get to Arkansas?" they asked together.

Their daddy stopped unpacking and sat down on the floor. Jondavid and Andrea sat down with him.

"God didn't come to Arkansas," he told them.

"Not even in an airplane?" Andrea asked.

"God was already here," said Daddy. "God was here in Arkansas even before Arkansas was here. God was here before there were any people or any houses."

"Was God here before the trees?" asked Jondavid.

"And the grass?" asked Andrea.

"Yes; God was here before the trees and the grass because He made the trees and the grass—and the rocks and the hills, too."

"And He made the dirt," said Jondavid.

"And the rivers," added Andrea.

"But, I thought God lived in Delaware," said Jondavid. "We talked to Him there."

"God does live in Delaware," said his daddy. "God lives everywhere because He is God. He heard your prayers in Delaware, and now He can hear your prayers in Arkansas, too, because He is God."

"No matter where we are, God is close to us," said Mother as Andrea climbed onto her lap. "Tomorrow we are going to a new church. We will sing and we'll pray and we'll hear our new pastor tell us about God's love for us. God is everywhere, and His love is everywhere."

Andrea yawned and rubbed her eyes.

"Someone is sleepy," said Daddy.

"Time for bed," added Mother.

Jondavid and Andrea kissed their daddy good night and climbed into their beds.

"I'm glad God is everywhere," said Jondavid.

"Me too," added Andrea. "I love Him."

"He loves you too," said their mother. "Right here in our new house in our new town in Arkansas, God loves us."

"Good night," said Jondavid and Andrea as their mother kissed them and turned off the light.

"Thank You, God, for loving us in Arkansas," prayed Jondavid. "Thank You for loving us everyday. Amen."

A Second Chance

by Judy Rouse

Franklin wondered how slowly he could walk. He could see the classroom door at the end of the hall. He could hear the girls giggling already. He tried walking one step forward and four steps back. His Sunday school class-room was getting farther and farther away, when he felt a warm hand on his shoulder.

"I think you want to go this way, Franklin," Mr. Lopez said. Franklin didn't want to go that way at all. In fact, he wanted to go home and play in his fort.

Last night, he and Bobby were just putting the last branches on the roof of their fort when he heard Mother calling.

"Franklin, time to come in now. Remember, we have church and Sunday school in the morning."

"Aw, Mom, come on; we just got the fort finished. Can't I please stay out a little longer?"

"I'll give you just five more minutes. Then I want you in the tub."

Franklin turned to his friend. "Let's hurry, Bobby. We still have time to get our baseball cards and canteens out here."

Franklin hurried into the house, found his baseball cards and filled his canteen. He had just crawled back into the snug fort when he heard, "Franklin, Franklin! Time to come in now."

"Mom, just a little more time . . . ple-e-e-a-s-e."

"Franklin, you heard me! I already gave you five more minutes. It's time for you to come in—now!"

Franklin groaned.

Mother's voice cut through the air. "Come in now, Franklin! Right now!"

Franklin snail-walked to the house, slunk into the bathroom, and slammed the door. He turned on the water full force. It splashed on the floor and towel cabinet. He was glad. He ripped off his clothes, dropped them in a pile and jumped into the tub. He made some splashing noises, hopped out and grabbed a towel, put on his clothes and headed for the family room. His favorite show was on.

"Franklin," Mother called. "Come back here and wipe up the floor, wash out the tub, and hang up your towel."

Franklin did not move from the TV.

"Franklin! Do you hear me? Come here this instant!"

Franklin scurried to the bathroom, dabbed at the floor, gave the tub a once-over, and threw his towel over the bar.

He ran back to the family room and dove into his bean-bag chair. Only a few seconds later he heard, "Son, it's time for bed. Remember, it's church in the morning."

"But, Dad—my show isn't over. Just five more minutes, please?"

"Son, don't argue with your father. It's time—now."

"Please, just five more . . . "

"Now, Franklin!"

Franklin stormed off to bed. He dropped his clothes, put on his PJs, and crashed into his pillow. When Mother came in for his good-night kiss, Franklin just aimed his cheek her way.

"Don't forget to say your prayers," she said as she closed the door. Franklin thought, "No way! I'm not saying any prayers. I wish there was no church tomorrow. I wish I never had to go to Sunday school and church again."

But now it was Sunday morning and he was stuck. Mr. Lopez, Franklin's Sunday school teacher, had his hand on Franklin's shoulder. There was no escape.

After roll call, songs, collection, and the opening prayer were finished, it was time for the lesson. Franklin was still brooding. It didn't help when Mr. Lopez asked Franklin to read the lesson. It was the story of Jonah. Franklin read as he was asked.

Jonah received a message from the Lord. "Go to the city of Nineveh. Tell the people there that I am going to destroy the city because of its wickedness."

Jonah said that he would go to Nineveh, but he was afraid. He ran away. He got on a ship in order to hide from the Lord.

The Lord sent a great storm. The sailors were afraid. They asked Jonah, "What can we do to stop the storm?"

"Throw me into the sea," said Jonah. "I know that God sent this storm because of me."

The sailors picked up Jonah and threw him overboard. Then the storm stopped.

The Lord sent a huge fish to swallow Jonah. He was inside the fish for three days and three nights. He prayed inside the fish. He promised never to worship another God; he gave thanks to the Lord for being alive; and he promised to go to Nineveh as he had said he would. So the Lord made the fish spit up Jonah onto the beach.

This time, Jonah obeyed the Lord. He went to Nineveh and told the people, "Forty days from now, this city will be destroyed."

The people were sorry for their sins and gave up their sinful ways. God saw that they had changed, so He changed His mind and did not destroy them.

Franklin sat back in amazement. Even then, in Bible times, when people disobeyed, God tried to bring them to their senses.

"Mr. Lopez," Franklin asked, "does God always scare people first before He forgives them?"

71

"No, of course not," Mr. Lopez replied. "Usually He uses peoples' consciences or other people to remind them of their need for His forgiveness."

Wow! Franklin thought. That's just like what Mom and Dad do. God just wants me to take His forgiveness. Jesus can forgive me even when I don't obey my parents or come happily to Sunday school.

Franklin prayed for forgiveness that morning. He said he was sorry and asked God to forgive him. Then Franklin began to feel good—good about being in Sunday school, even with all those giggly girls and Mr. Lopez.

Franklin still couldn't wait to get home to his fort and Bobby, but he knew he was in the right place, right where God wanted him on Sunday mornings.

Maybe he and Bobby could sleep out in the fort tonight. Now that would be a real adventure!

The Baby in the Bulrushes

by Phydella Hogan

The sun shone hot among the thick bulrushes along the great Nile River. Miriam was gathering reeds for her mother, Jochebed, to weave into baskets. She tossed a handful on the pile beside the path and decided that was about all she could carry. Wiping the sweat from her face, she pulled some long stems of marsh grass, tied them around the bundle and lifted it to her shoulder. My, it was heavy! But it wasn't far to the house, and then she would watch her baby brother while her mother worked.

A rustling sound in the weeds beside the path made her pause, her heart pounding. Spies were everywhere since the wicked new king had ordered all baby boys killed. The sound didn't come again, so she hurried on.

So far, no one knew about her baby brother—at least *she* hadn't told anyone. But he was three months old now, and it was hard to keep him quiet. She remembered last spring when her friend, Sarah, had told about a new baby in her family. Sarah hadn't said "brother," just "baby." That night the soldiers came and took him away. The family never saw him again. In spite of her load, Miriam began to run.

Panting, Miriam threw her bundle by the door and raced through the house. They kept the baby behind the curtain that hid Miriam's bed. As she peeked in, she had to clap her hands over her mouth to keep from shouting with joy. The soldiers hadn't found him yet! Her mother had just fed him, and now his curly head rested on her shoulder, the big brown eyes almost closed. Miriam watched his long lashes dip like tiny feathers to his rosy cheeks. He was instantly asleep.

He was so adorable, Miriam thought. How could anyone want to kill him? And the poor little thing didn't even have a name. Once, Miriam had asked her father, Amram, what the new baby's name would be. He had answered almost angrily, "What use to give him a name when he will never grow up to use it?" Then Father had stalked out of the house with tears in his eyes.

Miriam always had kept her bed smooth and neat before the baby came. Now, as Jochebed laid him down and gently pulled up the covers, Miriam began tossing toys and pillows helter-skelter, under and on top of the covers. If the baby lay still and didn't cry, anyone looking in might think he was just another lump on an untidy bed.

It was Miriam's job to keep him quiet while her mother worked. Usually, he gurgled and cooed happily. When he cried, Miriam would wrap a soft cloth around her finger, dip it in a mixture of honey and water, and let him suck the cloth. If that didn't work, she would try to make enough noise to cover the sound of his crying. She would sing, jump up and down, drop things on the floor— anything to make a racket until her mother could come and take care of him. Jochebed kept an eye on windows and the door, and, if someone was coming, she would begin to hum loudly. This was the signal for Miriam to jump into bed, pull up the covers, and pretend to be asleep. Anyone looking in would see a small girl taking a nap in an untidy bed. If the baby didn't cry or move, he would look like just one more lumpy bump under the covers— Miriam hoped.

Jochebed said, "Until the baby wakes, you sort reeds while I weave."

As they sat by the door working, Miriam asked, "Mama, why does the king want to kill our baby?"

Her mother sighed, picked up a handful of reeds, and began weaving. "Because we are Hebrews, and our baby is a boy."

"What's wrong with being a Hebrew?" asked Miriam.

"Nothing," answered her mother, "but the king is afraid of us. God brought our great-great-grandfathers from Canaan to Egypt many, many years ago. The first one was Joseph, who was kidnaped in Canaan as a young man and sold as a slave."

While they worked, Jochebed told how Joseph soon gained the king's confidence because he was able to explain the king's puzzling dreams—that there would be a great drouth and famine after seven years. So, the king put Joseph in charge of buying up grain during those seven years and storing it until the time of the famine. When it did come, all the other countries were starving, but Egypt had plenty. Soon, everyone was coming to Egypt to buy grain. Joseph's brothers from Canaan also came. Joseph was glad to see them and asked the king's permission to allow his father and his eleven brothers and their families to live in Egypt.

When they arrived, the king soon saw that, like Joseph, they were good workers, honest and dependable. They raised huge fields of wheat, oats, and barley. Some of them brought flocks of sheep, goats, and cattle. Over the years they built roads, irrigation ditches, houses, and bridges. The rich Nile Valley grew green and prosperous, and the dozen families grew into hundreds and hundreds of families. God blessed them, and the king liked them and treated them fairly.

But the present king, Miriam's mother continued, is cruel and greedy. He took all the herds and the farm products for himself. He passed harsh laws and made slaves of the people, working them long, hard hours at the hardest jobs. Some of them began to grumble, and the king realized that there were more Hebrews than Egyptians, and that they were bigger and stronger. He became afraid. That was when he passed the law to kill all new-born baby boys. If they couldn't grow up, then they wouldn't become a danger to him and try to take over his kingdom.

While her mother talked, Miriam watched her nimble fingers flying among the reeds. The basket was taking shape rapidly. Miriam thought it was too long for a bread basket, and it didn't look like a laundry basket. "Oh!" she exclaimed, "that looks like a little boat."

Her mother smiled. "It is. Maybe we can keep your brother safe in it for a while."

"But, if you put him in the river, he will float away. Or the little boat might tip over and he would drown." Miriam was horrified at the thought.

"We won't put him in the main part of the river," said Jochebed. "We will hide him in the reeds at the edge of the side pool where the king's daughter comes to bathe. But first, we have to make this basket watertight." Together, Miriam and her mother filled every tiny crevice with tar and pitch until no water could get through. Then they lined the basket with soft cloth and made a small pillow. Their creation looked like a beautiful toy.

Early the next morning, before the sun was up, they placed the baby in the basket and carried it between them to the pool. The baby was still asleep when Jochebed kissed him, then pushed the basket, baby and all, in among the reeds at the pool's edge. "Stay with him," she told Miriam, "but not too close. If anything happens, come and tell me." Then Jochebed quickly ran toward home.

Miriam stood shivering, jumping at every noise. No soldiers were allowed near the pool where the princess bathed, but if the baby cried, someone would be sure to hear him. "Oh, please, God, don't let him cry," she prayed. "Don't let anyone tell a soldier where he is."

Miriam shifted from one foot to the other, watching the basket, watching the palace a hundred yards away for movement, listening fearfully to every tiny sound. What would she do if someone did come near? She didn't know. The air began to warm as the sun rose higher.

What was that?

Footsteps!

Peeking through the reeds, Miriam saw the princess with several of her maids coming toward the pool. The princess wore jewels at her neck and waist, on her fingers and in her hair. How they sparkled in the sun! Her robe shimmered with every step she took. How lovely she was! Even the maids wore beautiful clothes. When they reached the side of the pool, the maids undressed the princess, chattering softly all the while. They helped her into the water and, with soft brushes and fragrant soaps, began bathing her. There was much splashing and laughter. Miriam almost forgot about the baby until the basket swayed and sent little ripples into the pool. Miriam felt her heart jump so hard that she thought it might leap right out of her throat and land beside the baby.

The princess noticed the ripples, too—and spied the basket. "Look!" she exclaimed. "Someone has sent me a present. Quickly! Bring it to me!"

When the maids brought the basket, the princess raised the cover and peered in. The baby's face broke into a smile, and both little fists waved furiously. In wonder, the princess reached in to touch him. His soft hand curled around her finger. "A baby!" she exclaimed. Pushing the basket ahead of her, she waded ashore, the baby still clinging to her finger.

"Quickly!" she shouted. "Help me dress! Someone find a nurse! I will keep this baby."

"But he is a Hebrew," protested a maid.

"Do as I say!" snapped the princess. "Hurry! He may be hungry."

As the maids scrambled for clothes, Miriam slipped from the reeds and knelt before the princess. "Please, Your Highness, I know a nurse," she said.

"Good. Bring her immediately. I will pay her well."

Miriam ran home faster than she had ever run before. Her mother was lying on the bed, crying bitterly. "Mama!" Miriam screamed with joy. "The princess found the baby and wants you to come take care of him."

Jochebed and Miriam ran all the way back to the pool. The princess handed the baby to Jochebed. "Take care of 'my' child until he can eat solid food. Then bring him back to me. His name is Moses because I took him out of the water. I will make sure the soldiers don't bother you." She started to walk away, but turned back. "And see that you treat him well. I will be visiting from time to time."

Miriam and Jochebed smiled at each other. Carrying the little "prince" and his basket, they walked home, thanking God. On the way, Miriam asked, "Mother, do you think God planned for the princess to find our baby and keep him alive?"

"I'm not sure," replied Jochebed. "We'll have to wait and see."

Home Again

by Muriel Steffy Lipp

Ellie's adventure was over—almost. She had gone to Brazil, all by herself, just two weeks ago. Her aunt had met her at the airport in Rio de Janeiro. Now she was back in the U.S.A., here in Kennedy Airport in New York. But I might as well be in China, she thought to herself. These airports all look alike. The flight attendant with daffodil-colored hair had just led Ellie off the plane and now was taking her . . . where? Where were her parents? They said they'd meet the plane.

"Where are my parents?" Ellie asked the attendant.

"Oh, they'll be along."

"What if they're late? Or what if they don't come?"

"I'll stay with you until they come." The stewardess smiled at Ellie through straight, even teeth. She was very pretty and had kind eyes.

Crowds of people roamed the airport. Most of them were speaking English, and Ellie enjoyed hearing her own language again. In Brazil everyone spoke Portuguese. Aunt Luisa and Gilda had spoken English around Ellie, but when they weren't talking to her, they spoke Portuguese.

The flight attendant helped Ellie get her suitcase, and then a man had to check it to see if she had anything in it she was not supposed to have. Customs, they called it. She worried about the purple stone her cousin had given her. It was beautiful, but she wasn't sure she was supposed to have it. The man didn't mind about the stone. In fact, he didn't even look inside her suitcase.

Then the flight attendant told Ellie to sit down on a bench. She'd be right back.

How long, Ellie wondered, was "right back."

Ellie felt lost. Where were Mom and Daddy? Did they forget about her? What if they never came? All the time she was in Brazil, she never had forgotten about them. When it was bedtime at Aunt Luisa's house, and she was in the big bed with her cousin, Gilda, she never fell asleep without praying for Mom and Daddy. Sometimes the pillow got a little wet because she missed them so much. Did they miss her? Maybe she loved them and needed them more than they loved her. If not, why weren't they here?

Ellie watched the people hurrying, hurrying—this way and that. Some of them were hugging and holding hands. They all had suitcases. An old woman had her arm around a girl Ellie's age. Was that the girl's grandma? A man was holding a baby up high over his head. The baby was laughing. Was that his baby?

Jesus, Ellie prayed, please let Mom and Daddy come soon. I know You love me and took my sins away. And, I know You're with me. But, I'm scared. Please help Mom and Daddy find me soon.

Ellie pulled her jacket around her shoulders. It was cold here in New York. When she had left Brazil, it was so hot she had wanted to pack the jacket inside the suitcase. But Aunt Luisa had said, "Nao, nao. It's cold in New York. You carry it."

Ellie remembered all the things that Aunt Luisa had done for her in Brazil. Aunt Luisa was married to Mom's brother, Frank, Ellie's uncle. They had taken Ellie on a trip up a river to a jungle. She had seen wild parrots squawking from the trees. Cousin Gilda had said there were big anaconda snakes in the jungle. Ellie had hoped they wouldn't see one. They hadn't.

Ellie had learned to eat many new things. She had tried everything, even though she didn't like them all. She didn't like the black beans they often ate, but she did like those sweet fruits—mangos and papayas. And, it was fun chewing on sugar cane, though they said it was bad for her teeth.

"Ellie!"

Ellie turned her head and, before she knew what was happening, Daddy was picking her up and hugging her. Mom kissed her three times and then looked at her and kissed her again. Daddy and Mom were just the same, and Ellie guessed they still did love her.

Just then the flight attendant returned. "My parents are here," Ellie said. "Thanks for helping me."

"Did you like Brazil?" Mom asked.

"Oh, yes! I saw parrots in the jungle and ate mangos and papayas and I got a purple stone from Gilda and . . . "

"Wait a minute," said Daddy, laughing. "You don't have to tell us the whole two weeks in one minute. Let's go somewhere and have a bite to eat."

Daddy took the suitcase, and Mom and Ellie walked with their arms around each other.

"Thanks, Jesus," Ellie prayed silently. "It's wonderful to be home."

Moondreams

by Phydella Hogan

I went to sleep and had a dream
Of riding through the sky—
With God—upon a moonbeam;
And, oh, we went so high!

We almost touched the twinkly stars;
We crossed the Milky Way
And drank from the Big Dipper—
I wished that I could stay.

I made a bag of silken clouds—
Shimm'ry, soft and blue—
And filled it up with stardust
To bring back home to you.

I made a wish on every star
As through the sky we sped.
Then, sliding down my moonbeam,
I landed safe in bed.

I woke and thought about my dream
Of riding through the air,
And how I hadn't been afraid
For God was always there.

He made the clouds, the sun, the moon;
He made each shiny star.
They shine for me; they shine for you—
No matter where we are.

And God is with us every night;
He's with us every day.
He watches us when we're asleep
And when we go to play.

So, say your prayers; jump into bed
And close your sleepy eyes
And dream of flying high with God
On moonbeams through the skies.

All Grow'd Up

by Lois Zimmermann

"Binny, wash your hands and come downstairs. Your daddy's home, and dinner is almost ready."

Mrs. Ellis put the finishing touches on the salad, opened the oven door, and reached for the casserole.

Bang! Crash she heard in the hall.

Still holding the pot holders in her hands, she ran to the hall in time to see her husband helping five-year-old Binny to her feet. Binny was safe and sound after her tumble down the stairs, but the sight of her face made Mrs. Ellis gasp.

Binny looked as though she had dipped her face in flour. A bright pink circle covered each cheek, and her lips were smeared with gooey pink lipstick. Her blond hair, piled on top of her head in a wispy bun, resembled a dandelion. She had put on her frilly pink petticoat and had tucked her mother's black lace shawl under the elastic band to hold it in place. Bracelets covered both arms, and a long string of blue and white beads hung down below her waist. One high-heeled silver shoe was still on the stairs. The other lay in the hall.

"I guess I have to practice more in high heels before I walk downstairs again," Binny said, trying not to cry.

Mr. and Mrs. Ellis tried to look cross, but they both burst out laughing.

"Why are you laughing at me? I thought you'd think I was pretty and all grow'd up." Tears rolled down Binny's cheeks making little streams in the powder that covered her face.

Mrs. Ellis hugged her little daughter. "Now, now, it's all right. We'll talk about all this after Daddy cleans you up. I'll finish making supper."

A short time later, Mr. Ellis and his daughter, now scrubbed clean and wearing her pink pajamas and robe, seated themselves at the table. They all bowed their heads and folded their hands while Mr. Wllis said the blessing.

After Mrs. Ellis served the dinner, Mr. Ellis began. "Binny, you could have been hurt very badly falling down the stairs, and we're thankful Jesus kept you safe. But, it was naughty to put on your mother's clothes and jewelry and to use her make-up. Why did . . ."

Binny interrupted, " 'Cause I want to be all grow'd up like Mommy and Melissa next door. I'm not a baby any more, and I don't want to be called 'Binny.' That's a baby name. I want to be called 'Belinda' and dress up and have fun like grow'd ups do."

"But, Binny—Belinda. Melissa is sixteen, and you're only five. You'll have to wait. That's the way Jesus planned for people to grow up."

"But I don't want to wait 'til I'm sixteen. That's forever away. So I'm going to hurry it up. I'm gonna pack up all my toys and have a room like Melissa's—with a bul'tin board and pitchers out of magazines on it, and then you'll see how grow'd up I am."

"You're packing up all your toys? What about Muggsy?" her mother asked in surprise.

"Oh, I won't pack Muggsy away. She sleeps with me."

"But won't she be lonely without her dolly friends? What about them? Who will tell them Sunday school lessons and give them rides in their buggy?"

Binny looked puzzled. "Well-l-l, maybe I won't put my dolls away."

"What about your cousin, Jimmy? What will you two play with when he comes to visit?"

"I guess I should keep out the little cars and the telephone that talks back. He likes that. Don't you think Jimmy's almost old enough to be called James?"

"He seems to like being called Jimmy," her daddy answered. "We thought you liked being called Binny. Using nick names is one way of showing love."

"It is?" Binny looked surprised.

"Yes, your mommy and I love you as you are now—and so does Jesus. And we'll love you just as much when you are ten or twelve or sixteen. But think of all you would miss if you were suddenly sixteen."

Binny looked thoughtful for a moment. "What would I miss?"

"M-m-m," Dad said slowly. "Probably your toys and playing tag and jumping rope and doing projects in Sunday school. Grown-ups just get to sit and listen and sometimes talk, but you get to do projects, like the manger scene you put together last Christmas. And, you'd miss wearing a funny costume on Halloween; Melissa doesn't wear one any more."

Suddenly Binny looked worried. "May I be excused?" she asked. "I have to tell my dollies I'm not going to put them away. They were sad this morning when I told them I wouldn't be playing with them any more."

As she ran into the hall, she called back, "It's all right to call me Binny."

Disciples at the Zoo

by Gloria A. Truitt

Laura squirmed in the seat belt, trying to see more of the passing roadside. "Daddy, are we almost there?" she asked.

"Well, we're one mile closer than the last time you asked," he answered with a wink, "but we still have another hour to go."

It was a long drive from northern Michigan to the Brookfield Zoo in Chicago. Though Laura tried to be patient, the trip seemed to be lasting forever.

"I have an idea," said Mother. "Let's play a game to help the time pass more quickly."

"What kind of game?" asked Laura.

"Let's find things along the road that begin with the letters in the alphabet," suggested Daddy. "You go first, Laura. Do you see anything that starts with the letter A?"

"Apples!" yelled Laura as they passed a fruit stand. "Now it's your turn, Mother. You find letter B."

Mother spotted a big barn for B. Then Daddy pointed to a cornfield for a C. Then it was Laura's turn to find something that started with D.

Miles later, Laura was still searching the roadside, but there were no dogs, ducks, or anything that started with D.

As they rounded a curve, Laura saw a man changing a flat tire. Another man was helping him. "Disciple!" shouted Laura. "I see a disciple!"

Mother knew what Laura meant, but Daddy looked puzzled. "Where's a disciple?"

"See that man helping the other man? The helper is the disciple," said Laura. "Each time we do a good deed, we are doing God's work. Jesus said that everyone will know His disciples by the love they show one another."

"You're right," said Daddy, "but how did you learn about discipleship?"

Laura explained that, the week before, she had seen an elderly lady drop a bag of groceries in a parking lot. "Eggs splattered on the blacktop, and cans rolled beneath parked cars—and do you know what, Daddy? Everyone walked past without stopping to help—everyone except me."

Daddy listened quietly as Laura continued. "When I got home, I asked Mother why those bad people hadn't stopped to help. She told me they weren't bad, only thoughtless. Then she read Jesus' words to me from the Bible."

They were miles past the two men changing the flat tire when Laura finished her story.

"Well," said Daddy, "I guess you did find letter D after all. And, now, I've spotted letter E—the entrance to Brookfield Zoo."

"Hooray, hooray!" shouted Laura, and the game was quickly forgotten.

The zoo was everything Laura had imagined. First they took a train ride around the zoo, stopping to see a herd of bison that roamed the "Western Prairie." They watched dolphins perform in a giant tank, and they laughed at Olga, the walrus, with her bristly whiskers and jutting tusks.

While watching a polar bear pace back and forth, Laura rested her right foot on the bottom railing of the fence. As she leaned over for a closer look, her knee slipped through the vertical iron bars. Oops! She tried to pull it out, but couldn't. With a frightened look, Laura called to Daddy, "Help! My knee is stuck!"

"Now, don't get excited," Daddy said calmly. "I'll get your leg out of there." He stooped down and tried to pry her knee from between the bars. But, no matter how hard he tried, Laura's knee wouldn't budge.

By now, a large group of people had gathered around, each suggesting a different way to free her leg. One man said, "Twist her knee to the side and then pull it out." But that only forced her leg farther between the bars.

A pretty lady with red hair said, "Why don't you straighten her leg, then pull it out." But that didn't work either.

Now everyone was concerned. Tears filled Laura's eyes when a stranger patted her head and said, "Don't cry, honey. When I was your age, I got my leg stuck in this fence too—and look," he grinned, tapping his knee, "I still have it." In spite of her tears, Laura smiled at the stranger and then started to laugh.

After a few more tugs and pulls, Daddy glanced up at Mother. "You'd better get help from the first-aid station. Her knee is starting to swell."

Mother hurried down the path and found a zoo policeman with a walkie-talkie on his belt. She told him what had happened, and together, they ran back to Laura. The policeman took one look at Laura's leg, then pushed the button on his walkie-talkie. "We have a little girl caught in the fence in front of the polar bears," he said, winking at Laura. "Can you send me some extra help—on the double?"

Within a few minutes another policeman arrived, carrying a paper cup. He hopped the fence to the other side, smiled and asked, "Are you feeling okay?"

"Uh-huh," Laura answered shyly, "but, what's in the cup?"

"This happens to be the best remedy for stuck knees," he said with a chuckle. "It's popcorn oil from the stand across the way." Then the policeman removed Laura's shoe and sock and smeared the oil around her knee. "Well, that did it!" he said as Laura's leg slipped out from between the bars.

Laura and her family thanked the crowd and the two policemen for their kind help. As everyone waved goodbye, Laura looked up at Mother and Daddy and said, "I knew I'd see a lot of animals here, but I never expected to meet so many disciples at a zoo!"

By this all men will know that you are my disciples, if you love one another.

—John 13:35

One Small Candle Aflame

by Sharon Beth Brani

Let your light shine before men, that they may see your good deeds and praise your Father in heaven.
—Matthew 5:16

"Elizabeth, Elizabeth!" The sounds of a neighbor child's voice calling outside could be heard within Miss Belle's house. "That Elizabeth," she chuckled to herself. "She is so full of life and fun. She's a joy to have in my Sunday school class. Everyone wants to play with Elizabeth."

That was true. Elizabeth's giggles and shouts of laughter could be heard all over the neighborhood. From morning till night, Elizabeth was busy—running, riding her bike, roller skating, and playing games with the other children.

Elizabeth began the first grade at school that fall. Along with the other children, she enjoyed learning to read and spell and do number problems. She brought in exciting things for show-and-tell. One time, she had a real snake, and the whole class broke forth in screams of fear and delight. Wherever she was, there was fun.

Elizabeth was often the first one to arrive at her Sunday school class. When they would read the Bible story aloud, her hand was always the first one raised to volunteer. She was eager to learn about Jesus, and she especially enjoyed hearing about the way He touched people—the blind, the deaf, the young and the old.

One Sunday, Elizabeth did not show up for class. Her chair was empty. Miss Belle stood in front of the class and quietly said, "Boys and girls, Elizabeth will not be with us today. She has had an accident and is in the hospital."

The children looked at each other with fear in their eyes. They waited in silence for their teacher to tell them more.

"Yesterday, Elizabeth was standing near two boys who were playing with a BB gun. She accidentally got hit in the eye."

During the Bible story time, the children tried to pay attention, but they couldn't keep their minds on the lesson. They were thinking about Elizabeth. Their eyes were drawn to her empty chair. When they were dismissed, no one felt like running and laughing.

For the next few Sundays, the boys and girls in Miss Belle's room were unusually quiet. They wondered if Elizabeth would ever come back. One Sunday, Tommy, the boy who usually sat beside Elizabeth, asked, "Miss Belle, is Jesus going to make Elizabeth die?"

Miss Belle looked at Tommy and then at the whole class. "No," she said, "Jesus is going to make Elizabeth well again, but the doctors were not able to fix her eye that was hit. They are going to make her an artificial eye instead. Jesus will help the doctors do it. She will be back to Sunday school soon. You'll see."

The boys and girls looked at each other. They remembered the Bible story about Jesus touching the blind man's eyes—and he could see. They remembered that Jesus took the Centurion's daughter's hand—and she became well again. But—would Jesus touch Elizabeth, they wondered.

"Yes," Miss Belle answered, "but we already know that He won't fix her old eye. That's gone. However, we also know that Jesus loves Elizabeth and will help the rest of her get well."

The next Sunday, Miss Belle said, "Next week Elizabeth is coming to Sunday school."

"Yeah!" yelled the boys and girls. It seemed as if their bubbly friend had been away for years!

That morning, the children excitedly planned a surprise for Elizabeth. With Miss Belle's help, they decorated a big box and filled it with brightly wrapped gifts.

One week later, the first-graders bounded into the room and took their seats. Where was she? Their eyes kept looking at the door. How would she look, they wondered. Would she still be full of fun and laughter? Would she be able to run with them and think of new games to play?

Shortly after ten o'clock, the door opened and Elizabeth slowly walked into the room with her father. She kept her eyes down and busied herself hanging up her jacket.

Very quietly her father whispered to Miss Belle, "She should be fine today, but she says she can't read. Her other eye works okay, though. If you have any problems, please let me know."

"Elizabeth will be fine, I'm sure," smiled the teacher.

After her father left, Elizabeth quietly went to her chair. Her head hung. Her blond hair only partially covered the big white patch. She could feel the eyes of the other children on her, and she desperately wanted to avoid their curious stares. Miss Belle finished taking the attendance. The room had never been so quiet!

Then, before the Bible lesson was told, Miss Belle stood in front of the class. "Elizabeth," she said softly, "we are all thrilled to have you back. We've missed you, and the boys and girls have a surprise—just for you."

Elizabeth slowly lifted her head to look at her teacher. Her one visible eye showed fear, embarrassment and pain.

"Would you come up to the front of the class and sit in this chair?" Miss Belle smiled encouragingly. Slowly, Elizabeth got out of her chair and walked to the front of the room where a big rocking chair had been placed. She sat on the chair, keeping her head down.

"Today, Elizabeth, you are going to be our queen for the day," said her teacher as she placed a brightly-colored paper crown on Elizabeth's head. "And now, we have some gifts for our queen to open."

Elizabeth watched as Miss Belle carried in the big box. Elizabeth still had not said a word. The other children waited. Miss Belle reached into the box and pulled out the first gift. She handed it to Elizabeth and said, "It's from Tommy."

"Thank you, Tommy," whispered Elizabeth. Slowly, she began to take off the wrapping paper. When she saw the two coloring books and the new box of crayons, her mouth turned up in a small grin.

"I think Elizabeth is lucky," said one girl.

"I do too," echoed a few others.

"Well, you wouldn't-a liked what happened to me," responded Elizabeth.

Gradually, as she opened each present, Elizabeth began to relax with her friends and to talk about the accident. She described the plastic ball that was inserted into her eye socket and would eventually be replaced with a glass eye. Of course, since she wore a patch, it would be several weeks before the children could see the ball.

"Now, children," Miss Belle said, "because it's hard to see with just one eye, I thought it would be fun if we all wore a patch this morning."

So, one by one, Miss Belle taped a white patch over one eye of each of the children. Elizabeth looked on with amusement. Even Miss Belle wore a white patch.

Elizabeth went back to her chair and listened to the Bible story. "Who will read the next page for us?" asked Miss Belle.

Elizabeth quickly lifted her hand to volunteer. Miss Belle smiled. When they had finished, Elizabeth looked at her teacher and grinned, "I didn't think I could read any more—but I can."

"Yes, you can. Jesus has touched you and healed you in a very special way. You still can do everything you used to."

It took a while, but Elizabeth gradually learned to live with only one eye. In time, she found that she could do anything her classmates could—ride bikes, swim, play games, and even shoot baskets. But, best of all, her thankfulness to Jesus showed everyone that life was still great—and that Jesus is still touching people.

Wish upon a Falling Star

by Frances Carfi Matranga

I saw a star slide down the sky
So quick, so very bright!
Within a moment it was gone,
Completely out of sight.
Yet while it glowed I made a wish
That I might ever be
A light that shines for Jesus Christ
As He's a light for me.

A Robin from God

by Gwen Ardis

Todd lay on the sun-warmed grass beneath a maple tree and looked high into the branches. He saw that the robin's nest was still nestled there, but could no longer hear the noisy chirps of hungry baby birds.

He turned away with a sigh. The baby robins were gone. They had left the nest. A lonely feeling came over him until he felt his pet cat, Darcy, softly rub his leg.

Todd reached for a small stick and wiggled it in the grass. Darcy pounced at it playfully until, out of the corner of his eye, the cat saw something else move—something much more intriguing than a stick. He flattened his body against the ground and fixed his gaze beneath the branches of a dense bush. The pupils in his green eyes grew enormous as he prepared to pounce.

Todd let out a shattering scream. "Darcy! No!" he yelled. With a lunge, he grabbed his cat and held him tightly. After he had locked Darcy in the garage, Todd returned to the bush. He pushed back the branches and peered into the shadows. Huddled there, in a small feathery ball, was a frightened baby robin.

With the tiny bird cradled in his hands, Todd hurried to the house. "Mom," he called out, "I found a baby robin, and he can't fly yet. Darcy almost caught him, so I'll have to keep him," he added breathlessly.

His mother agreed that the baby robin needed a temporary home. She decided that the small storage room would be perfect. She lay newspapers on the floor and covered boxes with old sheets. "Just remember," she cautioned Todd, "when the robin learns to fly, we have to let him go."

97

"I know, I know," Todd repeated excitedly. The speck-led robin squirmed in his hands, trying to get away. "Don't worry, baby robin," he assured the bird, "I'm going to take good care of you." It was then that Todd gave his new pet the name Baby-robin.

After the robin was settled in a small box, Todd headed for the garden with a spade and an old tin can. He knew that robins loved worms. When he had dug up several, he eagerly carried them back to the house. But Baby-robin fluttered wildly and would not eat.

With an unhappy sigh, Todd turned to his mother. "Why won't he eat? I know he's hungry."

"Baby-robin must learn to trust you," his mother replied.

"How can I make him do that?" Todd asked.

"The same way Jesus teaches us to trust Him," she answered; "by working patiently with us as He reminds us of His love." She smiled encouragingly. "Talk softly to Baby-robin. Let him get used to your voice."

"Mom," he said, squinting his eyes seriously, "I'm sure about one thing. I'd never ever hurt Baby-robin. I love him too much."

She put her arms around his shoulders. "Unselfish love is wonderful, isn't it? It means God's unselfish love is alive in our hearts."

"I don't think it's alive in my cousin Tommy's heart," Todd replied, shaking his head. "Tommy is mean to animals."

"Only God can be sure of that," his mother said. "Maybe it's there, but not very strong, yet."

"But, it makes God happy when we want it, doesn't it?"

"Very happy," his mother agreed.

Todd settled down on the floor cross-legged. He faced Baby-robin and began talking to him. Then he dangled a worm above the bird's head. Baby-robin trembled in fright and would not look up.

But Todd was patient, and Baby-robin finally fixed a beady eye on the tempting worm. He could not resist it. Opening his yellow beak, he swallowed it in one big gulp.

During the following days, Todd wore a path to the garden, digging worms and feeding them to Baby-robin. As soon as Baby-robin would hear footsteps in the hallway, he would hop out of his box and greet Todd at the door. His loud chirps seemed to say, "I trust you, Todd, and I'm ready for dinner."

One morning, Todd's mother had a suggestion. "We can't let him hop forever. It's time to give Baby-robin flying lessons," she announced.

Todd giggled. "Aw, Mom, how can we do that?"

"We'll trick him into it," she said with a laugh. "Watch."

First she placed Baby-robin on top of a box. Then she walked to the opposite side of the room and held up a worm. As soon as Baby-robin saw the worm, he eagerly hopped along the box toward it. When he came to the edge, he instinctively spread his stubby wings and fluttered them.

Todd cheered him on. "That's it, Baby-robin. You can do it."

Baby-robin took off, making a hasty and lopsided landing on the floor directly below him.

It took another day before Baby-robin could fly from one side of the room to the other. He even learned to land on Todd's shoulder. Sometimes the little bird would peck gently at Todd's earlobe or at the buttons on his shirt.

Every night, Todd would take his reading book into the storage room. Baby-robin would fly over and perch on his shoulder. (Todd felt that he read better when Baby-robin looked at the book with him.)

Day by day, Baby-robin's wings grew stronger and stronger. "He flies great, just like a big bird," Todd said one morning. Instantly, he regretted having said the words. He knew exactly what his mother was thinking.

"Yes, Todd. It's time to set him free."

"Just a little longer," Todd pleaded. "He's still a baby, even if he can fly."

"The longer we keep him," she warned, "the less chance the mother robin will take him back. The outdoors is where Baby-robin belongs. He needs to be in God's world of trees and sky, else he'll become a sad little bird."

After school that day, Todd noticed several big robins in the yard. Slowly dragging one foot after the other, he shuffled toward the storage room. Baby-robin heard him coming and greeted him with loud and happy chirps.

Todd picked him up and pressed him close. He rubbed his cheek against the soft feathers. "I don't want you to go, Baby-robin," he whispered. "I want to keep you forever."

His eyes were swimming with tears as he carried Baby-robin outside and carefully set him on the ground.

At first, Baby-robin did not move. Then he seemed to recognize his own special world. There was green grass all around. Big trees reached high into a beautiful blue sky. As chirping sounds came from his throat, a mother robin heard him. She flew over and popped a fat worm right into his beak.

Baby-robin hesitated as he watched the mother bird fly across the street. Then, spreading his own wings, he flew gracefully after her and disappeared from sight. Tears dripped from Todd's cheeks as he ran into the house and upstairs to his room.

When his mother came up later, he was stroking Darcy, who was curled close against him.

"Mom," Todd said as his mother sat down beside him. "I thanked God for letting Baby-robin find his mother."

His lower lip trembled. "I know I'm lucky to have Darcy," he continued, "but I miss Baby-robin. And it hurts here," he said, patting his chest.

His mother smoothed back his rumpled hair. "Love is like that," she explained. "It gives us so much joy, yet it can also bring hurt, even when it's love for a tiny bird."

Todd sat up suddenly, a faraway look in his eyes. "Maybe God gave me the robin so I'd remember how much Jesus hurt." He looked up into his mother's face. "Jesus loved us enough to die on a cross for us, didn't He?"

"That's right, Todd," she nodded. "He chose to die in order to give us eternal life."

Todd snuggled closer to her as a smile spread across his face. "Mom," he said, "now that God knows that I can love more than one pet, maybe He'll give me another bird. Or, maybe a rabbit or a raccoon." An impish grin made his dark eyes sparkle. "Or, how about a baby bear?" he giggled.

His mother laughed with him. Then, with a swoop of their arms, they gave each other a happy hug.

Stage Fright

by Pat Holt

On a beautiful Sunday morning, the sun was shining and the birds were singing, but Kevin didn't care. He was not happy.

"Kevin," his mother called, "time for breakfast. I've fixed your favorite kind of pancakes—blueberry. Come and get it." But Kevin didn't care about pancakes this morning. He just picked at his food. He knew what was going to happen today at Sunday school.

"Kevin, darling, you've hardly touched your breakfast," his mother said. "Are you feeling all right?"

"No, Mommy," Kevin answered. "I'm not feeling very well. I don't think I'd better go to Sunday school today."

His mother touched his forehead gently. "You don't seem to have a fever. Where does it hurt?"

"My tummy." Kevin's mother told him to lie down for a while on his bed until his tummy felt better, but Kevin knew that it would never feel better if he had to go to Sunday school. The truth was, Kevin did not want to go. He was afraid. He knew what the class was going to do, and he did not want to do it.

Kevin lay on his bed with his hands behind his head, looking at the ceiling. The worst thing was going to happen at Sunday school. The class was going to practice in the big auditorium for a program. Yuk! The teacher had told the children that they would have to walk alone down the long aisle up to the stage; then walk alone up the steps of the stage; then stand there with everybody in the whole Sunday school and all the mommies and daddies and grandmas and grandpas looking at them.

But that wasn't the worst part. Kevin was going to have to say a Bible verse in front of everybody—all by

102

himself. He was too scared to do that. Kevin knew he couldn't do it.

Kevin's mother came into the room. "Are you feeling better now?"

"No," Kevin answered firmly. "I'm not feeling any better. My tummy still hurts. I don't think I'd better go today."

"Well, I know how much you love Sunday school, so your tummy must really hurt," his mother concluded. "Yes, you can stay home today, Dear, and rest."

Right away, Kevin's tummy felt better. His face lit up with a big smile. He was not sad inside. Good! Now he wouldn't have to say that verse on the stage in front of everyone.

Ten minutes after his mother left the room, he still could smell breakfast. He jumped off his bed and went to the kitchen. "Mommy, my tummy feels better now. May I have some pancakes? I think I can eat them now."

"Of course you can, Kevin," his mother answered and gave him a big plate of pancakes, dripping with butter and syrup.

After he finished his plate, he was ready to play. "Mommy, may I go outside and play with Kitcat?" he asked.

"Are you sure your tummy is okay, Kevin?" his mother asked.

"Oh, yes! I feel real good now, Mommy."

"I see," she replied. "Yes, you may go outside—but we have to go someplace first." She reached for her purse and car keys.

"Where are we going?" Kevin asked.

"Well, since you are feeling so much better, let's go to Sunday school. We'll only be a few minutes late."

Oh, no! That's not what Kevin wanted at all. His stomach started to hurt again, and he said, "Mommy, I just can't go today. My tummy just started hurting again— real bad!"

Kevin's mother sat down beside him. "Kevin, you love Sunday school. I don't understand what is happening today. Please tell me what's wrong. Maybe I can help."

Now, Kevin knew that his mother loved him a lot. Maybe if she knew the truth, she would not make him go to that bad practice. So, he told her the whole story.

Kevin's mother took him on her lap and kissed away his tears. Then, she gently asked him, "What Bible verse do you have to say all by yourself?"

"It's from Exodus 15:2, Mommy, and it says, 'The Lord is my strength.' "

Kevin's mother smiled. "That's a wonderful verse, Kevin. Do you know what it means?"

Kevin shook his head no.

"Well, I think if you know what it means, you might be able to go to the practice without a tummyache."

Kevin began to cry again. He clung to his mother's coat. "No, Mommy; I can't do it. Please don't make me!"

"Just listen, Kevin," she said and gave him another hug. "Think of your Bible verse. Do you know who the Lord is?"

"God . . . Jesus?" Kevin asked with a trembly voice.

"That's right. And when it says He is your strength, it means He makes you strong enough—brave enough—even to go up on a stage and say your verse all alone. Jesus will give you the courage to do that, Kevin."

"But, I just can't," said Kevin, whimpering.

"That's why Jesus is always there to help us," his mother reminded him. "Whenever He asks us to do something, He also helps us do it."

Kevin just listened.

"Jesus will help you not to be afraid or scared. Why don't you try asking Him with a prayer?"

"Will He really help me not to be scared?"

"Of course," said his mother.

So Kevin prayed, "Dear Jesus, You know how really scared I am, but Mommy says You'll make me brave—like You promised in my Bible passage. So, help me do a good job and not be afraid. Thank You. Amen." Kevin turned and gave his mother a big hug and kiss.

"Do you feel better, Kevin?" she asked.

"A little, but I'm going to keep asking Jesus to help me—especially during practice time."

That morning at the practice, Kevin's tummy did not hurt. He asked Jesus to help him not be afraid going down the aisle, and he wasn't. Kevin asked Jesus to help him not be afraid when he said his verse, and he wasn't.

But the best part was the day of the program. Kevin, dressed up in his Sunday clothes, walked down the long aisle and up the big steps onto the stage. He said the verse loudly and clearly. He was not afraid. He knew that Jesus had helped him to do a very good job.

Stop Sign

by Muriel Steffy Lipp

"Jamie, you stop throwing stones, or I'll report you!" yelled Della, her forehead wrinkled in anger. Della was the new fifth-grade patrol.

"It doesn't hurt nothin'," said Jamie, heaving another stone at the stop sign across the street. He had lived in this neighborhood all his life. He wasn't about to let a newcomer tell him what to do, even if she was a grade ahead.

"That does it!" said Della. She wrote something on a page of her looseleaf notebook.

Jamie loved baseball. In fact, he was pretending a hard toss from the outfield as he pelted the stop sign with stones. He continued until the "H" bus came, and all the kids from the Fourth-and-Vine neighborhood got on.

Bus "H" dropped the children at the front door of Fourth Street Elementary, and Jamie, his blue backpack heavy with books, plodded down the hall toward his classroom. He put his jacket away and hurried to his seat. Ms. Crandall let the Bus "H" kids play games until the other buses and the walkers arrived.

"You're going to get in trouble for throwing stones this morning," said George, jumping one of Jamie's reds in checkers.

Jamie shrugged.

It wasn't long before the other buses arrived. Then, when Jamie was almost winning at Concentration, Sarah pushed at him and said excitedly, "Mr. Arturio wants you out in the hall."

Jamie sighed and hurried out the door. The hall was filled with kids going to the school store, the office, or wherever they always went first thing in the morning. They moved quietly now because of Mr. Arturio.

"What's this I hear about you throwing stones at the bus stop?"

"I wasn't hurting anybody—just seeing if I could hit the stop sign," said Jamie, defensively.

"What is the rule about throwing stones?"

"I don't know."

"What is the rule about obeying your patrols?"

"He's supposed to," said Della, who now was standing beside Mr. Arturio, "but he didn't. I told him to stop, but he kept right on throwing."

Jamie bowed his head. He hated that she was so goody-goody, always ready to tell on a guy.

"I'll send home a note to your parents," said Mr. Arturio. "You bring it back with your parents' okay for you to stay after school tomorrow."

Jamie slogged into the classroom just as Ms. Crandall started calling attendance.

George whispered to Jamie, "What'd he want?"

"Nothin'!" Jamie tried to hold back the tears that were oozing out.

Then it was lunch count—then reading, language arts, math, P.E., lunch, social studies, music, and home.

Jamie didn't know how to give the note to Mom and Dad, so he just laid it on Mom's plate at suppertime. She read it and put it down. "Let's say grace," she said, reaching out so that the family could hold hands.

After the prayer, Mom passed the note to Dad, while Jamie took some chicken and mashed potatoes.

"Is this true?" Dad asked.

Jamie nodded his head.

"Then we'll sign it," said Dad, "and you stay after school tomorrow."

"I can believe you were throwing stones," Mom said, "but why didn't you stop when the patrol said to?"

"Della's a namby-pamby! Anyway, I was only throwing at a stop sign. That didn't hurt anybody."

"But," said Dad, "I bet it nicked the paint on the stop sign."

"And," Mom added, "what if you'd hit a child by mistake?"

Jamie really felt picked on when his sister, Mary, who was in junior high, joined in. "What if everybody started throwing stones at stop signs?"

Jamie made a face at Mary.

"Now, Son," his dad said. "What you did was wrong, but we forgive you—and so does Jesus. Don't ruin that by starting a fight with your sister."

Jamie got the point. He just felt overwhelmed with all of them jumping on him.

At bedtime, Dad came into the room. "I was like you," he said, lowering his tall body to sit on the bed. "I used to toss everything I could lift—stones, balls, acorns, and persimmons. We had a persimmon tree outside our house. Once I threw a persimmon at a car. The car window was open, and I hit the driver. He stopped the car and marched me right in to my parents."

"Wow!" said Jamie. "What did Grandma and Grandpa do?"

"I don't remember," said Dad. "But that was the last time I threw a persimmon at a car."

"Dad—one thing. Everybody tells me I can't throw anything. What can I throw?"

"Well," said Dad, stroking his chin, the bed sinking down where he sat, "let's see. Balls are to throw. We could check up on Little League. Maybe you're old enough for baseball."

"Or," said Jamie, pulling himself up on his elbow, "first we could get one of those metal targets and hang it on the garage. I could throw rocks at it. I'd like that!"

Dad agreed that was a better idea than throwing at stop signs. But, he decided to put a large piece of plywood behind the target for the stones that missed. He didn't want the garage damaged.

As Jamie dozed off to sleep, he thanked God that his dad understood about having an itchy right arm, an arm that wanted to throw everything.

The Loving Gift

by Gloria A. Truitt

"Be sure to carry it with both hands," called Mother as Laura crossed the street, sniffing a box of freshly baked sugar cookies. Laura knew Mother was still watching, so she turned to give her a brave smile before ringing Mrs. Gilly's door bell. Laura wished her tummy would stop doing flip-flops as she waited for an answer. Laura really didn't want to deliver the cookies because she felt shy. She also felt a little frightened because she had never met Mrs. Gilly. Laura thought, what if she's a crab and doesn't like kids? Then she heard approaching footsteps, and the door opened.

"Well, well!" said a lady with twinkling eyes. Her hair was piled on her head in a mass of white curls, and her wrinkled face was creased in a broad smile. "Won't you come in?" she asked. "You're the little girl from across the street, aren't you?"

After Laura had introduced herself, she handed the cookies to the lady and followed her into a large, cheery room. Sunlight filtered through white lace curtains that framed each window, and in front of the windows dozens of glass shelves displayed hundreds of tiny cups and saucers. "Oh, they're beautiful!" said Laura.

As she gazed around the room, her eyes noticed a large, glass case near the end of the sofa. Laura didn't speak, but walked slowly over to the case. "What wonderful dolls!" she said. Then, without thinking, she blurted, "Do you play with these?"

"Well, in a way I do," chuckled Mrs. Gilly. "I've had them for a long time, and I guess you'd say these dolls are my hobby." During the next hour, Mrs. Gilly told Laura all about the dolls and their clothes and where they came from and why each one was special.

When it was time for Laura to leave, Mrs. Gilly thanked Laura for the cookies and said, "I hope you'll come back and visit me again."

Laura ran home and burst into the house. "Mother, Mother!" she called. "I had the best time with Mrs. Gilly! I was silly to be afraid of her. And you should see her doll collection!"

Mother gave Laura a big hug. "Slow down and tell me all about your visit."

"Mrs. Gilly told me so many exciting stories, I forgot about the time. I'm sorry I'm late."

"I understand," said Mother. "I knew where you were, so I wasn't worried. Now, tell me about the dolls."

"Oh, they're just wonderful!" sighed Laura. "Mrs. Gilly is 86 years old, and some of them are almost as old as she is. She keeps them on shelves in a huge glass case, and there's a story about each one of them."

At bedtime, Laura asked Mother if she could visit Mrs. Gilly again. "She's very old," said Laura, "and I think she's lonely. Besides," added Laura thoughtfully, "the Bible tells us that we should be kind to one another. I think Jesus would want me to be her friend."

Throughout the summer, Laura's visits to Mrs. Gilly became quite regular. Three afternoons a week, Laura stopped by to chat with her new friend; and each time, Laura returned with an interesting story to relate to Mother.

Laura told Mother about the lovely doll with the china head, and a very strange doll that was made from a corn cob. "The oldest doll still wears its original dress!" exclaimed Laura. "It was made by Mrs. Gilly's mother—and it doesn't have a single tear in it. Can you imagine that?"

Mother smiled. "I'm sure they are all beautiful, Laura, and I'm pleased that Mrs. Gilly has the time to tell you about them."

"Yes, Mother, they *are* beautiful. But the most beautiful doll is not very big or old, compared to the rest." Then Laura told Mother about a little black-haired doll with a pink gown and matching hat. "Her sister made the doll," said Laura, "and gave it to Mrs. Gilly on her sixty-fifth birthday."

Summer vacation ended and, although a new school year had begun, Laura did not forget her friend. As the weeks went by, Laura continued to learn more about Mrs. Gilly's dolls—but her favorite remained the tiny black-haired doll in the pink gown.

One Saturday morning, Laura woke up to find the ground covered with snow. As she bounced out of bed, Laura remembered that this was the day Father had promised to get their Christmas tree.

After breakfast, Father drove the family to the tree farm. They carefully inspected one tree after another until they finally decided on a beautiful Norway spruce. As Father and Mother tied it to the top of the car, Laura ran over to a small, but perfectly-shaped balsam fir. "Oh, *please*, could we get this one for Mrs. Gilly?" begged Laura. "She said she wouldn't have one this year—and this one would be just perfect for her."

"That's a wonderful idea," said Father, "and I'm glad you thought of it."

When the family arrived home, Mother and Father helped Laura carry the tree across the street to Mrs. Gilly's house. When Mrs. Gilly saw the pretty balsam fir, tears of happiness glistened in her eyes. "How can I thank you?" she asked, hugging Laura tightly.

"You don't have to," answered Laura, "because you are my friend—and this is a special time for love."

"You're right, Laura," said Mrs. Gilly, "for Christmas is the time to celebrate the greatest gift of love, the birth of Jesus Christ."

Father set the tree in a stand that Mrs. Gilly brought from a closet. Then they all helped to decorate it.

When it was time for Laura and her folks to leave, Mrs. Gilly said, "Wait a minute, Laura; I almost forgot to give you something." Quickly Mrs. Gilly picked up a brown paper bag from a table and, with a big smile, tucked it under Laura's arm. "It's a small gift," said Mrs. Gilly, "but I'd like you to have it as a little remembrance of our friendship."

At once, Laura knew what the bag contained, for the tiny doll in the pink gown no longer stood in the glass case. Laura cried "thank you, thank you" over and over again as she threw her arms around Mrs. Gilly. "This isn't small! It's the biggest gift I've ever had!"

At bedtime, Mother tucked the blanket beneath Laura's chin and kissed her good-night. With a big yawn, Laura sighed, "This has been a wonderful day, for now I know what Jesus meant when He said, 'It is more blessed to give than to receive.'" As Mother tip-toed from the room, Laura added, "Today I learned something else, too. There is no such thing as a small gift when it is given with love."

Bobby's Baby-sitter

by Karen Bigler

Bobby hated going to bed. Every time his mother told him it was time to go to bed and say good night, Bobby would cry, "Good night? Bad night!" He would whine, and he would cry. He would run the other way.

Bobby hated going to bed for a lot of reasons. That meant he had to stop watching his favorite TV show before it ended. Or, he had to put away his blocks just when he had them all standing in a tower. Or, he had to stop coloring the animals going into Noah's Ark. Or, he had to put away his puzzle before he had all the pieces in place.

Bobby hated going to bed. "I'm not tired," he whined.

"I'm thirsty. I need milk," he cried.

"My Hot Cycle is outside!" he screamed, and off he would go.

Bobby thought of one excuse after another . . . every night, every week. Bobby's mother was exhausted!

One night, Bobby had a new baby-sitter.

"Bobby's bedtime is 7:30," Bobby's mother told the sitter. "He hates going to bed, but do your best."

Bobby gazed up at the sitter and knew he'd get to stay up late tonight. "He'll never get me to bed," he thought.

The baby-sitter was a tall boy who had four little brothers at home. He picked Bobby up and placed him on his shoulders.

"Tell your mom good night," he said.

Bobby and the baby-sitter had a great time together. They drew pictures of airplanes all over the paper. They played Bobby's favorite game . . . and Bobby won! They read not one, but three of Bobby's favorite Bible story-books. They ate a dish of ice cream with chocolate sauce

114

on top! Bobby beat the ice cream with his spoon, making it all soft and creamy.

The sitter saw it was 7:00 and time to start getting ready for bed. He helped Bobby wash and brush his teeth. "Let's pretend your toothbrush is a street cleaner, Bobby." RRRRRRRRRrrrrrrr went the brush up and down each tooth.

"How'd you like to play another game?" he asked.

"Sure," yelled Bobby.

"Get on my back and I'll be a big camel" said the sitter as he got down on the floor. Bobby jumped up and held on tight as the sitter slowly swayed back and forth down the hall.

"Can you leap like a frog? Here, follow me." Bobby crouched down with his hands between his knees and jumped just behind him.

"Croak, croak" they said, leaping across the floor.

"Can you roll somersaults, Bobby?"

"Sure," he yelled.

"Show me how many you can do. One . . . Two . . . Three . . . Four. Good for you!"

"It's time for a bedtime prayer, Bobby," said the sitter kneeling on the floor.

"Thanks, God, for my new baby-sitter," Bobby said softly. "And, thank You for Jesus, who forgives my sins. In Jesus' name. Amen."

"We better wheelbarrow you to bed, now. Stretch out on the floor so I can grab your feet. Then, walk with your hands just one at a time."

"Good going!" cheered the sitter. Bobby fell into bed, exhausted as ever. He looked up at the sitter and said, "Good night." The clock on the wall showed 7:30 sharp. The sitter just smiled and said, "Don't let the bed bugs bite."

When Bobby's mother returned, she was surprised Bobby was tucked in tight. She paid the sitter and thanked him so much. How did he ever do it? she thought.

It wasn't until morning she learned the new trick, when Bobby asked, "Mommy, will you wheelbarrow me to bed tonight?"

A Bedtime Poem

by Eileen Spinelli

Soft comes the night;
"Hush," says the moon.
Shimmering stars
dance for you soon.

Snuggle you down,
cozy and deep;
Jesus' arms
hallow your sleep.

The Adventure of Lucy Lamb

by Pat Holt

If a man owns a hundred sheep, and one of them wanders away, will he not leave the ninety-nine on the hills and go to look for the one that wandered off? And if he finds it, I tell you the truth, he is happier about that one sheep than about the ninety-nine that did not wander off. In the same way your Father in heaven is not willing that any of these little ones should be lost.

—Matthew 18:12–14

A very long time ago there lived a pretty little white lamb named Lucy. She had bright eyes, a cute nose and four small, fast feet. It was Lucy's cute nose and four small, fast feet that got her into a lot of trouble.

She lived on a sheep ranch with her mommy, daddy, five brothers and sisters, and a lot of other sheep families.

Her shepherd, Caleb, was a very kind and gentle man who loved his sheep and called each one by name. He took very, very good care of them. His sheep ranch had the greenest and best grass to eat, and had a very nice fence around it to keep the sheep from going outside. Outside the fence, the grass was dry and brown. If the sheep ate that kind of grass, they would not grow up to be strong, but might get sick—and might even die.

Also, wolves and coyotes lived outside the fence. They liked to eat sheep, especially little lambs. At night, when the moon was bright and yellow, Lucy could hear the wolves and coyotes howling. She didn't like that loud, scary sound, and she would snuggle up to her mommy and daddy. Then the shepherd, Caleb, would come and pet her with his strong but gentle hands and say in a soft voice, "That's all right Lucy. I will protect you. I will take care

118

of you. I'll never let anything bad happen to you." Then Lucy would feel much better, close her eyes and go to sleep.

One morning, Lucy scampered over to where her mommy was and began to eat the green grass. Then she was ready for a big drink. So she scampered over to a cool, clear pool of water and took a long, refreshing drink.

All that eating and drinking made Lucy feel like playing. She went over to her mommy and nudged her. Her mommy gave Lucy a frown. I guess Mommy doesn't want to play, Lucy thought. She still wants to eat.

Lucy scampered over to her daddy and nudged him. Well, he wanted to keep on eating that wonderful green grass, too. So she went to each of her brothers and sisters. Each one gave her a little frown and went back to eating. Nobody wanted to play.

Then Lucy got an idea. She would go exploring all by herself. How exciting! She looked all around. All the other sheep were eating, drinking, or taking a morning nap. How boring! The shepherd, Caleb, was taking care of a sheep that had hurt its foot.

Lucy scampered off toward the edge of the sheep ranch, next to the fence. She looked at the fence. Then she looked beyond the fence. She saw some brown-looking grass and some big, old, dead trees. That would be interesting to explore, Lucy thought. I've never even touched brown grass before. I wonder what it feels like under my feet.

Lucy found a little hole in the fence. She pawed and pawed and made it larger until it was just big enough for her to wriggle through. When she was on the other side of the fence, she felt like a very big sheep and not just a little lamb.

Lucy looked all around. Then she began to walk. The brown grass felt different under her feet—dry and rough. She wondered what the brown grass would taste like. Her shepherd, Caleb, had told Lucy that the brown grass would

119

make her sick, but she decided that a little taste couldn't hurt. Lucy nibbled just a bit of it. Yuk! It was not nearly as good as the green grass she ate every day. She was glad she didn't have to eat dry, brown grass.

That little taste made Lucy thirsty, so she began to look for water. She walked and walked. There was no water in sight. So she walked some more—until she found a small, muddy pond next to some large, old, dead trees. The water didn't look good, but Lucy was very, very thirsty. She put her little pink nose close to the water. "Oh!" she scowled and backed away. "The muddy water even smells bad. I think I'll just go home and get a drink there."

Lucy looked around. She looked to the right, and she looked to the left. She looked in front of her, and she looked behind her. She didn't see the fence or the green grass or any other sheep or Caleb. Lucy was lost!

The sun was setting. Soon it would be dark. What could Lucy do? Where could she go? She had to get home. She was very tired and thirsty, and she was starting to get hungry. And, she was scared.

Lucy began to run. First she ran in one direction. She saw no sign of the fence or the green grass or Caleb, her shepherd. All she saw was more dry, brown grass. Then she began to run in another direction. Everything looked strange.

Now it was nighttime. Lucy heard the loud cry of a coyote. Coyotes like to eat little lambs, Lucy remembered.

Lucy was really, really scared now, and she started to run her very fastest. All of a sudden, in the dark, she stepped on something hard and sharp. "Ow!" she bleated. Oh, how it hurt! It was the worst hurt she had ever had. A sharp thorn was stuck in her foot. She couldn't get it out, and she couldn't walk. Lucy could only lie down on the brown, dry, cold grass and lick her sore foot.

"Oh, I wish I'd never left my mommy and daddy and my brothers and sisters and my shepherd, Caleb," Lucy cried. "I wish I'd never gone exploring on the other side of the fence. I don't like dry, brown grass and dead trees and muddy water. I don't like coyotes. I want to go home." She sobbed and sobbed, but there was no one to hear. Lucy was all alone for a very, very long time.

Suddenly she heard a sound in the dry grass. The sound was getting closer. Maybe it was a coyote come to get her and eat her. Lucy was so frightened that she began to shiver and shake.

Then she heard her name. "Lucy, Lucy!" It was Caleb, her shepherd, looking for her. Lucy bleated to let Caleb know where she was. Then she saw him. He looked down at her with kind, tender eyes. He bent down and gently took the thorn out of her foot. Then he lifted her into his strong arms and began to carry her back to the sheep ranch.

"Lucy, my little Lucy," Caleb said. "I counted my sheep tonight and found only ninety-nine. I know I have a hundred sheep, so I called each one by name, just as God calls His children by name—and you were missing. I have spent the night trying to find you, just as God does because He loves His children and will never, ever let one stay lost and away from Him.

"I love you, little Lucy, just as God loves each of His children—and I will always come to find you and get you. I will never stop loving you, just as God will never stop loving His children."

Lucy listened with her tired, half-closed eyes. She was so glad her shepherd would love her no matter what and would come to find her just as God does with His children. Lucy decided that she would never again go through the fence. She would never leave her shepherd, Caleb. She never wanted to be away from his love and care again.

Super Ball

by Muriel Steffy Lipp

Jedd was humming to let out the happiness from inside himself. He'd just found his old friend, the super ball. It was stuck between the heater and the wall. Jedd had been sitting there, crunch-crunching his cereal, when he spied this red dot under the heater. Oh, boy! The only thing better than a new toy is an old toy, lost and found.

He'd lost it after a high bounce several weeks ago. He'd looked everywhere, even under the heater. And now, here it was. He could bounce it on the way to school.

Jedd was the youngest of six children in his family. His mother and father both worked and left early for their jobs. And the older children had to leave for school before Jedd. So, Jedd was the last one at home.

He had to put away the milk after his cereal. Then he had to rinse his dishes. And it was Jedd's job to see that the front door was locked. Then he had to hide the key in a special hiding place in the shutter. And, of course, he had to remember his lunch money—and his books.

It was a lot for an eight-year-old to remember. But Jedd was getting good at it. He hardly ever forgot anything anymore. Mama was always praising him.

"Darling, you are my youngest," she'd say, "and you are so good at remembering. I pray for you at work. I tell Jesus, 'Now Jesus, Jedd is very young. Please help him to remember his lunch money. And please take care of him all day.' And Jesus does take care of you, and you're such a bright boy. For me, it's Thanksgiving Day every day."

Such talk embarrassed Jedd, but it also made him feel very proud. It made him want to remember all the time.

Jedd looked at the clock. Eight-thirty. He'd better go. Should he wear a sweater? His sister always called the Weather Bureau to find out the temperature, so he dialed the number, too. The weather lady said it was 70. No sweater.

He turned out the kitchen light. He grabbed his books with the lunch money lying on top. He locked the door and hid the key in the shutter. Then he patted the lump of super ball in his pants pocket.

Jedd skipped out through the backyard gate to the alley. This was his new shortcut to school. Maybe he would run into his friend, Bill. He could share the ball with Bill. Bill would take care of it.

As he walked, he bounced the ball. Isn't it fun to bounce a ball, he thought. I can hold my books in one hand and bounce with the other. Good catch, that's me! thought Jedd. Here comes an intersection. Stop and look both ways. No safety patrols in these alleys. I have to be careful.

Jedd could hear loud voices and laughter behind him. A group of older boys was heading for school. Jedd was going slowly because of bouncing, so the boys soon caught up with him.

"What you got there, Kid?" asked one boy.

"A super ball," said Jedd.

"Let's see."

Jedd showed him the ball, and the boy bounced it high and caught it. "Great!" the boy said. "I can use that. Thanks." And he walked off with the ball.

"Hey, that's mine!" yelled Jedd. "Give it back!"

The other boys laughed. They all walked ahead on their way to school.

Jedd began to cry. He thought of his mother and hoped she was praying for him. He was in trouble. What did Mama always say? "When you're in trouble, pray. Jesus is right beside you."

"Jesus, stay with me," whispered Jedd. "Don't go away."

Jedd hurried after the boys. He followed them to the big intersection across from school. Now there were lots of kids coming from everywhere. Jedd was glad for their friendly faces. He wasn't going to take that old shortcut any more. Up on the main street there were patrols who could have helped him.

He followed closely behind the boy with his ball. He followed him right up to the corner with the traffic light. The real friendly, laughing policeman was on duty today.

"Mister, that boy took my super ball," Jedd said, pointing.

"What's that? He took your ball? Well, let's see what we can do."

The policeman tapped the big boy on the shoulder and said, "Come over here, Buddy. Let's help this little fellow."

The policeman and the two boys moved to the side of the street. The cars took their turns crossing the intersection. Patrols held back the other boys and girls.

"Aw, take it!" said the big boy. He bounced the ball high in Jedd's direction and stalked off.

Jedd thanked the policeman.

"That's okay," said the policeman. "Now, if I were you, I'd keep that ball in my pocket until you get home. If he bothers you again, let me know."

Yes, Jedd thought; they might be waiting for me after school. Dear Jesus, You gave me help just now. Thanks for sticking with me. Please do the same for the rest of today. Amen.

The policeman stopped the traffic and stepped out to the middle of the street. Jedd took a run and a jump to catch up with his friend, Bill. "Hey," Jedd called. "You want to play super ball in my yard after school?"

Thommy Candato
and the Lizard's Tail

by Kevin Gingrich

"Can you give me a push?" Thommy Candato asked his mother. "I can't do it on my own."

Mrs. Candato took her son by the shoulders, aimed him, then gave him a gentle push down the sidewalk. The whirr of his roller skates vibrated beneath Thommy Candato's feet as he rolled down the rough sidewalk.

"I can do it all by myself, now!" Thommy called to his mother as he fought to keep his balance.

"I'll be here when you need me," his mother called back, and she went into the apartment building where the Candato family lived.

Outdoors, by himself, the Candato boy saw absolutely nothing. The whole world was dark to Thomas Candato—he had been born completely blind. But the blind boy felt the vibrations of the world rolling underneath his skates. He felt the morning sunshine warming his bare knees. And, every now and then, to keep his balance, Thommy touched one of the trees growing alongside the sidewalk. Then, down the walk he rolled.

Above the whirr of his roller skates, Thommy heard the voice of his neighbor, Dina Livingston, who usually teased him. "Come here," she taunted. "I've got something to show you, Thommy Candato."

Tommy rolled on down the sidewalk until he felt the presence of Dina.

"It's a present," said Dina, "for you."

"I bet!" Thommy Candato replied, grabbing a tree and cocking his head to one side.

Dina Livingston drew out her voice in a sneaky sort of way. "Trust me. Just put your hand out."

"Trust you-u-u?" Thommy tooted. "I wouldn't even trust you to give me a push!"

"Come on," urged Dina. "It's just a real neat biscuit."

A biscuit? thought Thommy Candato. He heard the sneakiness in Dina's voice, but he loved the feel of bread biscuits, so he stuck out his hand.

"Here!" said Dina, and she laid something in his hand. It had feet! Little, teeny feet that scampered up the arm of Thommy Candato.

"Ouch!" cried Thommy and, as quickly as a scared boy can, he shed the scampering "biscuit" off his arm.

"A lizard!" Dina hooted. "You thought it was a bread biscuit, and it was a lizard!" She screeched with laughter.

Thommy stomped off—chunk! chunk! chunk!—on his roller skates, going from tree to tree back toward his apartment. He did not think it was funny at all.

I'm not scared of an old "wizard," he told himself.

Dina yelled after him, "I found it under a rock—a squiggly, wiggly lizard," she sang, still laughing at Thommy.

Skating between two of the trees, Thommy heard her laughing at him. He got so angry that—whisk! whisk! chunk!—his roller skates went crazy, and down he fell.

"It hurts! It hurts!" Thommy cried, touching his bare knee. It felt sticky wet. "Blood!" Thommy gasped.

Thommy Candato crawled on the grass all the way home, his skates clinking behind him. "Mommy! Mommy!" he cried, melting tears rolling smoothly down both cheeks.

Indoors, Thommy asked his mother, "Does it need a big bandage?"

"I doubt it," said his mother, examining the hurt knee.

"Does it need a little one?" asked Thommy, hopefully.

"I doubt it," his mother replied.

"What does it need?" Thommy helplessly asked.

With her warm palms, his mother began to rub and squeeze Thommy's little bare knee just as she did when she was kneading bread dough. "A knee needs kneading; a knee needs kneading," his mother began to happily chant.

"It hooots," Thommy giggled.

"Oh, it does not," she said.

"But, what about the blood?" Thommy Candato giggled and gurgled.

"There's no blood," his mother assured him.

"Then, what's the sticky wet?" asked her blind son.

"A sucker," his mother told him. "Your little knee must have landed on a sucker."

"Prob'bly Dina Livingston's sucker," Thommy said sourly.

"Now what's the matter between you and your friend, Dina?" Thommy's mother wanted to know.

Thommy told her about the lizard. (But, he called the lizard a wizard.)

With her warm hands, Mother continued to knead Thommy's knee while she listened to the lizard tale. Thommy whimpered a little when he told the one part, about the ugly feeling of getting a lizard biscuit instead of a bread biscuit.

"Now, now," Thommy's mother whispered warmly. "Do you remember about Jesus?" She waited for her son to answer.

"Uh-huh," he whimpered.

"Remember how Jesus got hurt instead of you, instead of me, instead of Dina?" his mother asked kindly.

"Uh-huh," Thommy remembered with a whimper.

"And why did Jesus do it—for you and for me and for Dina?" his mother patiently asked.

"I can't remember," Thommy whimpered.

"Thomas," his mother said less patiently, "why did Jesus do it?"

Thommy answered with a final, short whimper, "To forgive me."

"And your mommy and your neighbor, Dina," Mrs. Candato added. "Jesus is the best friend we'll ever have."

Thommy was beginning to feel much better.

"Now, Thommy," said his mother, looking him in the eyes, "wouldn't you like to go back and see Dina?"

"*See* her? I'm blind," Thommy complained.

"Thomas Candato! You see more than most kids do," his mother said firmly. "Now, you roll right over to Dina's house and tell her you've forgiven her."

"Okay," Thommy said slowly. "But I can't get up."

"Oops," said his mother. "I forgot the yeast."

"What's that?" Thommy wondered.

"Yeast? That's what makes bread rise," said Mrs. Candato, and she pretended to sprinkle yeast on his knee— to make Thommy rise like bread dough.

"The sun rises in the y'east," said Thommy Candato.

"The sun rises in the *east*," his mother corrected. "Now, get up, Thomas Candato." Thommy's mother pulled him up and rolled him toward the door.

"Will it get a scar?" Thommy asked.

"Your knee? I doubt it," said Mother. "You're just exaggerating."

"Eggs-what-erating?" Thommy puzzled.

"Exaggerating," his mother explained. "That means you're making things seem worse than they really are. Now, off you go."

Out on the sidewalk again, Thommy rolled along from tree to tree on his way to forgive Dina Livingston. Whirrr-whirrr—he rolled under a tall tree that drooped its branches low over the sidewalk. One of the fingers of its branches reached down and, when Thommy rolled underneath it, scratched him on the head. It parted his hair right down the middle. Thommy grabbed the low branches and pulled himself to a crazy stop. "I forgive you," he told the tree.

Still clinging to the tree, Thommy stopped for a minute to think about the lizard. The tree was a good place to stop and think.

"That Dina Livingston!" Thommy protested to the tree. "How can she be my neighbor?"

Thommy felt for the tree's unmovable trunk. He looked up to where its big branches blocked out the warmth of sunshine, and his thoughts were turned toward Jesus and how He must have hurt. With the eyes of his fingers, blind Thommy Candato saw the deep, rough scars of the tree. "Bark," he said to the tree—and to anyone else who might have been listening.

"Wooof, wooof!" barked one of the neighborhood dogs, and it came padding along—click, click, click—on the sidewalk. Thommy pushed off the tree. He heard a quick and awful "yeeelp!" Thommy had rolled over the doggy's paw.

"Forgive me, Doggy," said Thommy to man's best friend. But the doggy just whimpered. Thommy remembered what his mommy had said—that God, who forgave, was man's true best friend.

On he rolled down the sidewalk. "I forgive you," Thommy practiced at the next tree (even though the tree had done nothing to Thommy Candato).

Three trees later, Thommy was at Dina Livingston's apartment. Chink, chink, chink—clumped Thommy up the stairs, with his roller skates on. He knocked at her door.

"You sound like a cricket—chink, chink, chink," Dina Livingston said when she cracked open the door. "Lizards eat crickets!"

"I forgive you," Thommy told her.

"That's okay," Dina said quickly. "I want to show you something."

129

Before Thommy could answer, Dina had wheeled him into the kitchen. "I have something for you in the refrigerator," she taunted.

"It's a 'wizard,' I bet," said Thommy Candato, "a lizard! And it's in your refrigerator."

"No, Thommy Can*dodo*," said Dina. "Lizards like it warm." She took Thommy's hand. "It won't hurt you," she said.

"I doubt it," said Thommy unforgivingly.

Dina laid Thommy's hand on something smooth and cold in the icebox. "It's just an egg," said Dina Livingston very sneakily.

"I know," said Thommy Candato.

Then he heard Dina jump back. "It's a lizard egg!" she screamed.

As fast as he could clump, Thommy rolled out of Dina's kitchen, out of her apartment, and—chink! chink! chink!—as far as he was concerned, out of her life.

He heard Dina laugh and laugh, her head poked out the kitchen window. "Thommy Can't-do-it! Thommy Can't-do-it!" she sang meanly.

"Thommy Candato's my name!" Thommy hollered, and he began to sing back just as loudly as Dina, "Someone's in the kitchen with Di-na; someone's in the kitchen, I know-oh-oh-oh . . . oomp!" Thommy had rolled smack-dab into Mister MacLean, his landlord.

"Whoa, there, young lad!" said Mister MacLean. "Where do ye believe ye're going in such a fine hurry?"

Mister MacLean had a deep, kind voice and strong arms. He held Thommy up as the skates tried to run away with Thommy's feet. Mister MacLean was as sturdy as a tree, and Thomas clung to him.

"Oh, that Dina Livingston!" Thommy complained. "She's just eggs-agitating." Thommy was about to complain to his landlord about the "wizard" and the "wizard egg" when he felt something on Mr. MacLean's chest.

130

"Why, Mister MacLean—you're wearing a necklace!" Thommy exclaimed, a little bit surprised to find a necklace on a man. "And, there's a *thing* on it."

"Ah," said Mister MacLean, " 'tis a very special thing on me necklace." He took Thommy's hand. "Feel it again, Thommy," he invited.

With his fingers, Thommy kneaded the thing on the necklace in the same way his mommy had kneaded his knee. "Ooh," said Thommy. "It's rough, it's rough. I feel the scars."

"Here," Mister MacLean brightened, and he took off his necklace and hung it around Thommy's own neck. "That'll help ye keep yer balance, Laddie."

"What is it?" asked Thommy, still fingering the thing on the necklace. The bottom part of the thing felt long and skinny and hard—like a lizard's tail.

" 'Tis the body of a man," said Mister MacLean, "a very wonderful man, at that!"

"Is he on a 'wizard's tail?' " asked Thommy Candato.

"No, Laddie," Mister MacLean answered in a winking sort of way. "He's on a tree, a kind of tree."

"A tree-e-e," said Thommy Candato, full of wonder, fingering the body on the tree. "I see. I see-e-e!"

"Ye mean yer mother hasn't told ye, Laddie?" asked Mister MacLean, very surprised indeed.

"I can't remember," said Thommy Candato. "You tell me again."

"Go, Thommy," his landlord commanded. "Have yer mommy tell ye all about Him, the man on the tree."

Thommy rolled back home, feeling the warm sunshine on his knees. The body of the man on the tree was beating against his chest.

Thommy showed the necklace to his mother. "Oo-o-o, Mommy," Thommy said in a slow, low breath. "He *really* fell! I can feel his scars."

131

Thommy felt his mother's arms wrap around him. She smelled nice and warm.

"That's all right, Thomas," she whispered. "He did it for you." And, then, Mrs. Candato told Thommy again all about the cross and Jesus, God's son, who died on the cross to forgive Thommy Candato and everybody—even Dina Livingston. Thommy could tell that his mother did not doubt it at all.

That night, outside, the tiny, invisible crickets hidden in the scars of trees went "chink, chink, chink." Inside, under Thommy's pillow, was the necklace with the Man who had climbed the tree. Mother had told him all about it—and Thommy would always remember.

The next morning, the sun came up in the east. Thommy felt it on his cheeks, and he rose to the fresh smell of warm biscuits, happily remembering that Jesus loved him.

The Invitation

by Therese Olson

Tony looked from the living room at his mom sitting at the kitchen table. She was making a list of relatives she wanted to invite to Daddy's birthday dinner. It was to be a surprise, so Mom was being very careful to keep it a secret. Tony had to be cautious not to say anything about the party in front of Daddy. That was really hard sometimes because he was so excited about his cousins coming over to play. A few times at the dinner table he almost said something, but Mom always warned him by gently kicking his foot under the table and giving him that you-better-not look. Soon Mom was done making the list and asked Tony if he would help her make the invitations tomorrow.

Sitting on the living room floor, surrounded by his trucks, Tony daydreamed about how much fun it was going to be having everyone there. He looked at his little sister, Katie, who was sitting on top of his favorite truck. Katie was only one year old, and Mom said she didn't know any better. Tony got the truck away from her, but then she started crying and ran out to Mom. Katie didn't care about parties or cousins or anything except her teddy bear—and messing up Tony's toys. Mom said that when Katie got to be five, like Tony, she would understand; but Tony had his doubts.

That evening at supper, it was Tony's turn to say the table prayer. "Thank You, Lord, for this find food that You have so well blest. Honor would bestow us, Lord, if You would be our guest," Tony prayed.Then he had an idea. Why not invite Jesus to Daddy's birthday dinner? When he helped Mom make the invitations tomorrow, he could make a special one for Jesus.

Tony could hardly sleep that night thinking about how surprised everyone would be when Jesus came to the door. Tony decided not to tell anyone, not even his mom, so that it would be a surprise for her, too.

That night, Tony dreamed about Jesus being at the party. He looked just like that picture in his Sunday school room, only it was Tony and Katie sitting on His lap. Katie had pulled His beard and dropped some of her ice cream on His robe, but Jesus only laughed. He sat right beside Daddy, and they talked about Daddy's work and about building the new garage Daddy wanted. Jesus told Mom that her supper was delicious and that she could win a blue ribbon. He told stories to everyone about His Father in heaven and His own love for everyone. Tony's aunts and uncles were all very quiet. Even Katie sat still while He talked. He sang Happy Birthday to Daddy with everyone. They all laughed when He asked if Daddy wanted "a pinch to grow an inch." Soon He said He must leave. Just before He left, He pulled Tony aside and thanked him for the invitation. He said not everyone would think of inviting Him, and He was very touched. He said He would see everyone again—and then walked out the door. Tony ran to the window, but He was gone.

Tony woke up early the next morning still thinking about his special Guest. Tony knew it was only a dream, but he thought that, when Jesus really did come to the party, everything would go just as in his dream.

After breakfast, Mom got out some paper, and Tony got his crayons and started making invitations to send out. Tony drew pictures on one side while Mom wrote the invitation on the other side. To help, Katie had a red crayon and made a scribble on each invitation so that everyone would know she had worked on them, too. After they were done, Mom put the invitations into envelopes and addressed them to send out. Then she put them into the mailbox for the mailman to pick up.

134

Tony took a piece of paper and his crayons to his room. He drew a picture of some clouds and angels. He drew a few trees and birds. He didn't know if they were in heaven, but didn't think Jesus would mind. He also drew a picture of his dog, Salty. Salty had been hit by a car and died. That had made Tony sad, and he had asked Daddy if Salty was in heaven with his grandpa. Daddy said he didn't know for sure, but if there was a dog heaven, Salty was probably there. On the back of his picture he wrote the best he could:

jesus
Cum to daddys burthday in ten
daes. I hop u liak the pictur.
Tony

Then he got an envelope and wrote,

jesus
heven

Tony wondered how the mailman would get it to Jesus. He thought for a minute, then decided to write "Air Mail" on the front of the envelope. He remembered his mom had written that on a letter she once sent and had told Tony that, when you write "Air Mail," the post office workers take your letter in an airplane to where it's addressed. Tony thought an airplane could probably fly it to heaven.

The next ten days seemed to last forever, but Daddy's birthday finally arrived. Tony thought a lot about his dream. He hoped Jesus had received his invitation and that He would come.

As everyone arrived, Tony kept running to the window, looking for Jesus. Tony began to worry. He walked to the corner and looked both ways—up the street, then down the street. Tony's mom called out the door that dinner was ready, for him to wash up.

As Tony walked toward her, she could see tears in his eyes. "What's wrong? Why are you sad?" asked Mom.

"It's a surprise, and I can't say," said Tony.

"Okay," answered Mom as she took his hand. They walked back to the house in silence.

While Tony washed his hands, he started to feel angry. Why hadn't Jesus showed up? That just didn't seem right. It was almost impolite.

Tony dried his hands and sat down at the card table where the cousins could all sit together. Everyone bowed his head as Uncle Don, Daddy's oldest brother, said the prayer. "Thank You, Lord, for this fine food that You have so well blest. Honor would bestow us, Lord, if You would be our guest."

Tony felt hot tears in his eyes. He jumped up from the table and ran to his room. Daddy called to him, but Tony didn't stop. Tony thought to himself, "Jesus never came! I wouldn't want Him to come if that's the way He's going to behave!"

Daddy followed Tony to his room and asked, "What's wrong, Son? Why are you crying?"

Tony blurted out the whole story between sobs—about the special invitation, how hard he worked on drawing his best picture. He told Daddy about the dream he had, and how happy Daddy was to have Jesus at his birthday.

Tony's daddy was quiet for a long time. Finally he put his arm around Tony and said, "Son, I'm very proud of you. You certainly did invite the most important guest. I know without a doubt that Jesus knows about your invitation and is touched that you thought about Him."

"Then, why didn't He come?" Tony asked.

"Oh, but He has," exclaimed Daddy. "You may not see Him like you can see me right now, but He is here just the same. When we ask Jesus to be a guest in our home, He is always gracious to accept. He is the invisible Guest who helps make our home a loving place. Jesus could let us see Him if He wanted. But He says, 'Greater is He who believes who hasn't seen than those who have.' It's not the right time for us to see Him, but He promises that we will someday. Until then, we accept Him as an unseen guest and believe. You know, Son, I believe He is right here in this room, feeling very happy that you invited Him to the party."

Tony looked around the room, wiped his eyes and smiled. He knew his daddy was right.

Tony went downstairs and ate his meal. Tony's uncles and Daddy all talked about their jobs and fishing, and Daddy told them about the garage he planned to build. Everyone told Mom how wonderful dinner was. Katie dropped ice cream on the floor, and rubbed chocolate cake in her hair, and everyone laughed. Tony played with his cousins and had a wonderful day. When the party was over, everyone went home.

Daddy took Tony aside and said, "Remember, now, what we talked about. Jesus never ignored your invitation, but was here the whole day!"

Tony hugged his daddy real tight and said, "Yeah, I know."

Talking to Jesus

by Gloria A. Truitt

I like to talk to Jesus when
    the day comes to an end,
Because He's shared the day with me;
    He is my closest Friend.

I talk to Him when I'm tucked in
    my cozy, comfy bed,
With Teddy Bear beside me and
    my pillow 'neath my head.

Although I cannot see my Friend,
    His caring love I feel.
No other friend could ever be
    so near to me and real.

Frederick's Friend

by Winifred Rouse Simpson

Frederick watched Mother wash his skinned knee. "It hurts," he said.

"You must have been running very fast."

"I wanted to tell you about the baby puppies."

Mother put a bandage on the knee. "Does that feel better?" she asked.

"Yes, thank you. Does God know I skinned my knee?"

"God sees everything you do, Dear."

"Then, why did I get hurt?" asked Frederick.

"God does not want His children to get hurt. He loves them. But, sometimes hurts happen. That is why God planned for big people to help the hurt go away."

"And," Frederick said before his mother could, "sometimes children don't do what their mommies and daddies tell them."

"That's true. And sometimes children don't use their eyes and ears. God planned for us to take care of ourselves, too," said Mother. "But, even when we don't, God watches over us."

Frederick thought for a moment. "God must get tired of all that watching. He has a lot to do. That's why I need a special friend—like a puppy. Then, if I get hurt, he'd come to get you. He'd be a special friend."

"Jesus is your special friend, Frederick," said Mother. "He forgives you when you are naughty, and He always watches over you. Plus, He never gets tired. He isn't like us. He doesn't need to rest. You can always depend on Jesus."

"Is that why we pray to Jesus?" asked Frederick.

"That's right," Mother answered.

"And can we talk to Him about anything?"

"Of course you can," said Mother. "Jesus wants you to talk to Him about anything you wish."

"Then I'll ask Him for a puppy."

"Are you sure you want to ask Jesus for a puppy?"

"But, I *need* a puppy."

"Many people think they need many, many things. But, some people trust Jesus to decide what they really need."

"But, how will Jesus know I need a puppy if I don't tell Him?"

"Jesus knows all about you, Frederick. He knows what you want and what you need. He knows what will be good for you. Jesus knows better than Mother and Daddy."

"How do I know Jesus will listen?" asked Frederick. "I can't see Him."

"No one can see Jesus with his eyes, Dear," answered Mother. "But, we don't need to see Him to know He is here."

"But how do I *know*?"

"Because He promised us in the Bible. Now, close your eyes and think a minute."

Frederick closed his eyes and waited.

Mother spoke softly. "All around us there is air and light. Outside the sun is shining. Flowers are growing in our garden. Inside there are a Mother and a Daddy who love Frederick very much. The fresh air and the shining sun and the love we feel for each other remind us that Jesus is with us. We don't need to *see* love to feel it."

Frederick opened his eyes and smiled at Mother. "Daddy said I should wait for a puppy until I was bigger."

"That's right," agreed Mother. "He thought it would be a good idea for you to wait until you can take care of a puppy by yourself. I'm busy taking care of a little boy who runs very fast and skins his knee."

Frederick thought some more. "Are there any special prayers to say about puppies?"

"I don't think Jesus needs a special prayer," said Mother. "He listens to you whenever you talk to Him."

"Then I will say, 'When I'm old enough to take care of a puppy all by myself, I would like to have one.' Will Jesus hear me if I say it that way?"

"Jesus will hear you, Frederick," said Mother. "But, remember, sometimes you might not get what you think you want. Will you remember that Jesus always hears you and loves you?"

"Even if I don't get a puppy?" asked Frederick.

"You can count on your Savior's love, Dear, whatever happens."

When it was time for bed, Mother turned down the covers while Frederick put on his pajamas. "I want to talk to Jesus," he said.

Mother opened the Bible and read, "Your Father knows what you need before you ask him."

"Thank You, Jesus, for knowing what I need," prayed Frederick. " . . . even before I ask for a puppy," he added in a whisper. Then Frederick closed his eyes and went to sleep.

The Truckers

by Reta Spears

George was sick of rules—rules at home, rules at school, even dumb rules in games. So when Uncle Dan asked Mom if George could ride along in his big 18-wheeler one weekend, George prayed like everything—then held his breath. "I think that would be just fine," his mom said—and George breathed again.

George didn't remember his own dad much. Mothers are nice, George thought, but a fellow just needs a big guy around sometimes. So whenever Uncle Dan's truck had a trip near by, he'd drop in and say, "Hey, George, how's my buddy?" Then they'd pretend to punch one another and goof around like guys do. George looked forward to Uncle Dan's visits.

But this was the best visit ever! George had ridden in the big truck before, but only a few miles each time. This time he'd ride for two whole days—like a real trucker. And there wouldn't be any dumb rules. Teachers couldn't yell, "No running in the halls!" Mom couldn't remind, "Bedtime at eight o'clock." And Jerry and Kevin couldn't say, "If you cross the line, you're out of the game!" George hated rules.

George tossed his overnight bag up to his uncle, who was sitting behind the steering wheel. "Trucker George" then grabbed the metal handle above the back wheel of the truck cab and pulled himself up to a foothold. He turned, gave Mom a quick hug, said bye in his most grownup voice, and scrambled into the open door of the cab.

Uncle Dan called to Mom over the noise of the engine, "Don't worry about us truckers, now. The Lord is traveling with us, and we'll be back tomorrow."

"I know," smiled Mom. "Now, have a great time—and obey all the rules," she waved as the truck began to roll forward.

"Rules!" muttered George to himself, but his grumpiness fizzled in the hiss of airbrakes releasing. George felt the engine rumble under him. His stomach felt 89 butterflies inside. Truckers George and Dan were on their way.

They turned onto a ramp to the highway, and Uncle Dan said, "Let's ask Jesus to help drive this truck, okay?"

"Yup," answered George and folded his hands on his lap.

"Kind of a little rule of mine," added Uncle Dan. George clasped his hands a little tighter. When Uncle Dan finished praying, George said an amen, then added, "What do you mean, 'rule'?"

Uncle Dan glanced at George and chuckled. "Oh, praying's not a rule," he said. "Just something important to me that I always remind myself to do."

"That's good," said George in relief, " 'cause I hate rules!"

"Well, say, now," said Uncle Dan, "truckers *do* have rules—and good truckers try to obey them."

George decided not to say anything about that. Instead, he asked, "Uncle Dan, could I climb back and ride in the bunk?"

"Sure," laughed Uncle Dan, "but take your shoes off so you don't get our bed dirty. That's the . . . "

"Rule!" finished George as he climbed back into the high sleeping area behind the seats.

The ride on the bed was smooth, and George felt safe and snug there. He could hear Uncle Dan better, too, above the noise of the truck engine.

From his perch, George watched factories glide by as he and Uncle Dan headed out of town. The few scattered farm houses began to show lights gleaming from their windows. It was beginning to grow darker.

Uncle Dan switched on the CB radio. "We'll just listen for a bit to see if anything important is happening," he said.

A voice from the radio crackled, "This is Red Fred. How 'bout a southbounder 18?"

George knew that "Red Fred" was the name, or handle, some trucker was using on the radio, but he wasn't sure about "southbounder 18."

Uncle Dan explained. "That means the trucker is looking for someone driving south on highway 18. If Red Fred is heading south, too, then they can sort of travel together."

Another voice came in clearly. "This is Dinosaur, southbound 18, heading into Mollie's for gas and dumplings. Bring 'er back."

George remembered that "bring 'er back" was one CB way to say, "It's your turn to talk." The mention of food also reminded George that he was hungry.

"Are we going to stop at Mollie's, too?" George asked Uncle Dan.

"Sure. Mollie's is a good truck stop. We'll eat there and bed down in the truck. Won't be so far to go in the morning."

Just then another voice cracked over the CB. "Breaker. I've got a ten-forty-two, mile marker two-0-three."

"That's an accident," whispered Uncle Dan as he listened intently.

The voice continued. "Gonna be a big traffic jam. Think the driver was going too fast."

George swallowed hard. "Uncle Dan," he said in the same intent whisper his uncle had used, "do you think anyone was hurt?"

144

"I don't know, George. The accident is behind us, but we can pray, can't we?"

"Sure," said George as he clasped his hands once again. "Dear Jesus," he began, "if anyone was hurt in that accident, please help them. And, help the drivers remember the speeding rules."

"I'll amen that!" said Uncle Dan. "Now, let's head toward Mollie's."

After supper Uncle Dan and George walked slowly out to the truck. George didn't say much, but he was thinking lots—about rules. They climbed up to the wide bunk, pulled off their shoes and crawled under the blanket. In a little while George said, "I thought there weren't any rules in trucks."

Uncle Dan said, "There'll always be rules, Partner."

"But, I hate rules!"

"How come?"

"I hate somebody always telling me what to do—then being mad at me when I goof. I bet nobody does that to truckers!"

"Hey, Partner," said Uncle Dan, "you've got it wrong. Truckers have lots of rules."

"They do?" asked George in disbelief, although he already knew the rule about speeding.

"Sure," Uncle Dan went on. "Truckers have rules about their rigs. They have to check everything for safety every day. The tires, the brakes, the 'fifth wheel' that holds the tractor and trailer together. Even the windshield wipers have to be checked. That's the rule."

"Okay, but . . . ," started George.

"And they have to keep 'logs,' books where they write down how many hours and how many miles they drive each day. It's the rule. If they drive too much, they can get too tired and fall asleep while they're driving."

"Wow!" said George. I never thought of that. They could have a wreck if that happened."

"You're right," continued Uncle Dan. "And there are rules about weight. Trucks can only carry so much weight on certain roads or the roads will wear out too soon. There are special scales that can weigh the whole truck every so often along the way. The signs at those places say 'Weigh Station,' but sometimes truckers call them 'chicken coops.' Truckers have to stop so their truck can be weighed by the Weigh Master. It's the rule."

"Wow," said George in wonder.

"Sure," said Uncle Dan. "There are even rules about the CB. We have to talk over certain air waves, and we're supposed to wait and take turns when we talk."

"I didn't know there were all those rules," said George.

"There are a lot more rules, too, and they all have a reason," said Uncle Dan. "But the important thing to remember is that you and I should always follow the rules because we're followers of Jesus."

"Oh, yeah," remembered George.

"Why do you think that's so?" asked Uncle Dan.

George said slowly, "Because Jesus said so?"

"Well, yes," said Uncle Dan, "but there's more to it. Jesus loves us and wants to take care of us. So, He put people in charge of us to do just that. So, whether we're obeying parents, teachers, policemen, or Weigh Masters, we're letting Jesus take care of us."

George thought for a minute, then said, "That's different."

Uncle Dan laughed and plopped a pillow on George's face. "So stop talking and go to sleep," he said in pretend gruffness. "We've got a big day tomorrow."

"Okay, Partner," grinned George in the dark. He'd have lots to tell Jerry and Kevin and Mom when he got home. But tomorrow he'd be a trucker for one more day.

Love for the Elderly

by Frances Carfi Matranga

Tammy loved greeting cards. They were so pretty, she decided to make some herself. Mother had given her a box of old magazines, ribbons, colored construction paper, and lace paper doilies.

"I love making things," Tammy told her mother. "But who can I make cards for? Nobody I know is going to have a birthday soon."

"How about friendship cards?" her mother suggested. "They can be sent to anybody, anytime."

"Good idea," said Tammy. Then she wrinkled her forehead. "But I see my friends almost every day when we play together. Do you know anybody who would like to get a friendship card?"

"How about the lady who lives at the end of our street?" said Mother.

"You mean Mrs. Grant?"

Mother nodded. "She was on her porch the other day when I went by. Poor lady. She looked so sad and lonely. But I stopped to talk to her. She invited me in for tea and was so happy to have company. It must be lonesome for old folks who live by themselves and can't get around much. We have at least four people like that on our street. There's Mrs. Grant and Mr. Pickwick and—"

"And Miss Smith and Mrs. Foster," Tammy added. "Once in a while I say hi to them."

"Mrs. Grant and Mr. Pickwick have no families to visit them or send them cards," her mother went on. "I'm sure they'd appreciate a friendship card from a little girl. You know, Dear, Jesus said what we do for others is like doing it for Him."

147

"That's what I'll do then!" Tammy exclaimed. "I'm going to make four cards. Thanks, Mama, for the good idea."

She got busy cutting, pasting, and writing. A couple of times she asked for help in spelling a name or a word, but other than that, she made the cards all by herself. When she had finished two of them, a green one and a pink one, she called her mother to come and see.

Mother looked at the green one first. It had rounded corners and folded down from the top. Tammy had pasted a small lace paper doily on the cover. She had cut out a colored photograph of a plate of cookies from a magazine and had pasted it on the doily. Attached to the top of the card was a tiny ribbon bow, and beneath that she had printed: HELLO! IT'S ME. Inside she had written:

Dear Mr. Pickwick,
> *I am thinking of you. Have a good day.*
> *I will visit you soon and bring some cookies.*

> > *Love,*
> > *Tammy Hart*

"Very nice," said Mother with a smile.

"Is it okay with you if we bake cookies for him?" Tammy asked. "And may I bring some to the other people I'm making cards for?"

"You certainly may," her mother said. "I'm proud of you for thinking of it. It'll be nice to bring them something. I don't believe Mr. Pickwick has had any homemade baked goods since his wife died last year. It'll cheer him up to know someone is thinking about him."

She picked up the pink card Tammy had finished. This one was square and edged with scallops of paper lace. On the cover Tammy had printed: THINKING OF YOU. With colored pens she had drawn little flowers all over the cover, front and back. Inside the card she had written:

148

Dear Mrs. Grant,
>*Flowers are sweet*
>*And you're sweet, too.*
>*I'll bring you a bunch*
>*When I visit you.*
>>*Love,*
>>*Tammy Hart*

Mother's smile grew wider. "Maybe you'll be an artist when you grow up," she said. "So you want to pick a bouquet of our garden flowers for Mrs. Grant, do you?"

"I didn't think you'd mind, Mom."

"Of course I don't mind. God likes for us to share what we have. Are you going to visit every one of the four people you're making cards for?"

"Yes," said Tammy. "They live nearby, so I'll just put the cards in their mailboxes. That way I don't have to worry about envelopes to fit. Then, after we bake the cookies, I'll bring them some. And flowers for Mrs. Grant to go with the poem I wrote for her. Let's make chocolate chip cookies, Mama. Everybody likes them."

"Chocolate chip it is," her mother said, looking pleased. "What you're doing is what everybody should do—show love for one another. That's what Jesus asks us to do."

"You gave me the idea," Tammy reminded her.

"But you're the one putting it into action." Her mother stooped to kiss her. "I'm sure your thoughtfulness will make the old folks happy."

And *that*, thought Tammy, made it all worthwhile.

A Helper for Jesus

by Jean Hegel

Tommy hurried into the kitchen, sat down at the table, and started to gulp his breakfast. He always looked forward to playing ball with his friends, and he didn't want to be late.

"Will you carry out the trash for me before you leave?" Mother asked.

"It'll make me late for my ball game," Tommy whined. "You know how I've planned and planned," he pleaded.

Mother said nothing. After a while she asked Tommy a question. "How did you like church yesterday?"

"All right, I guess. I liked Sunday school better. We talked about being a helper for Jesus." He layered his toast with jelly and shoved it into his mouth. "But, I guess I'll have to wait till I grow up to do that."

"Oh," Mother replied.

Tommy was almost finished with breakfast when his mother said, "I have another question. Remember when you got your baseball glove for your birthday? The first thing you did was go next door and play catch with Andy. Why?"

"Mom—a great gift like that's no fun if you can't use it with someone. Ya' gotta share it!"

"And what about God's gift of Jesus? You know, you're just like everyone else—sinful. Jesus doesn't have to forgive you or love you. But He does. Isn't that a gift worth sharing by being a helper for Jesus?"

"But, how can I do anything important enough to help Jesus? I'm only a kid," Tommy argued.

"Just think about this today. Whenever you see someone that needs love or forgiveness, think to yourself, 'I'll help Jesus and do it too.'"

"Okay," Tommy said with some hesitation, "but I don't think I'll have the chance." He left his dirty dishes on the table and didn't bother to push his chair back under the table. "We're gonna play ball this morning instead," he added as he grabbed his glove and left.

Once out the backdoor, Tommy heard a scraping noise on the walk. He saw his dog pushing an empty water pan, trying to get a little water to drink.

"I've not got time to get you a drink now, Laddie." As Tommy started out the gate, he remembered what his mother had said.

"Oh, all right. I guess God loves animals, too." He headed for the hose and filled Laddie's pan with cool water. The thirsty dog wagged his tail in appreciation and stopped drinking long enough to lick Tommy's hand with a very wet mouth.

Tommy wiped his hand on his pants and noticed the empty birdbath. He remembered that he was supposed to fill it yesterday. He sighed and pulled the hose to the birdbath and filled it with more cool water. "I guess Jesus would want the birds to have a drink, too," he thought, "but this has got to be all the good I can do today. I don't have any more time."

As he started out the gate, he heard his baby sister. "Bye, bye," she called to him and waved her little hand.

Tommy noticed that her shoe was untied. "Better have Mother tie your shoe, Little Sister. You'll trip and fall down." He stopped at the gate, laid his ball glove on the ground, and went back to his sister. As he leaned over to tie her shoe, she patted his head and giggled. Tommy carefully tied the shoes on her wiggling little feet. "There. Now you won't trip and fall."

"Tank you," she laughed and ran on to play.

"She is pretty cute," he admitted to himself.

Tommy closed the gate and went next door to his friend Andy's house. Andy grabbed his ball and glove.

151

"We'd better get going," he said as they hurried out of the house.

They had just started down the sidewalk when they saw Mrs. Brown struggling with her bag of groceries. "She sure walks slow, doesn't she?" Tommy said, noticing the cane she leaned on, clutching the bag of groceries with the other hand.

"My mom said that Mrs. Brown has a bad back that hurts a lot," Andy remarked.

"Let's help her carry the groceries," Tommy suggested.

"Do what?" Andy asked in amazement. "We'll never get to the game on time."

"I'm just trying to help Jesus today. Come on. It won't take long." Tommy hurried toward Mrs. Brown as a curious Andy followed.

"May we help carry your groceries into the house for you, Mrs. Brown?" Tommy asked politely.

"My sakes, yes. Of course you may." Mrs. Brown gladly handed the groceries to Tommy as Andy picked up another bag from the car.

"This is so nice of you, boys. I'll tell your mothers what gentlemen you are." She held onto the banister as she mounted the front steps one at a time.

"Call me anytime, Mrs. Brown. I'll be glad to help you carry things." Tommy was a little surprised at his own words, but Andy was wide-eyed at his friend's offer.

"Just a minute, boys," Mrs. Brown called. "I baked cookies. Have some." Mrs. Brown offered them the plate.

They munched their cookies as they went on their way. They were almost to the ball park when Tommy noticed two of his classmates teasing some little girls. They were holding a little kitten high in the air and wouldn't let the little girls have their pet.

"Give 'em the kitten, you guys," Tommy insisted.

152

"We won't hurt it. We're just having fun," his classmates argued.

"Just the same, you're scaring them. They're only little kids, and we're in the third grade." Tommy handed the kitten to the girls and hurried on as they smiled and waved to him.

Andy looked at his friend a little puzzled. "You're getting carried away with this helping Jesus stuff."

"It just seemed like the right thing to do," Tommy answered, a little surprised at himself.

Just then he noticed a boy he hadn't seen before leaving the ball field. He had his hands pushed deep into his pockets, and he kicked at some rocks as he walked away.

"Who's that?" Tommy asked one of his friends.

"He's a new kid. His folks just moved in down the street. He wanted to play, but he doesn't have a mitt."

Without hesitating, Tommy called to the new boy. "Hey! You can use my mitt. We can share."

"That's your new glove," Andy scolded. "Are you crazy?"

"It'll be alright. He can use it." Tommy waved to the grateful boy as he ran across the field to become part of the team.

Later, when the ball game was finished, Tommy returned home to find his mother starting out the door with a sack of trash.

"Here, Mom, I'll take that for you." He noticed a pleased expression on his mother's face when he started off the porch with the bag.

"Tommy," she called to him. "Jesus loves a willing worker—and mothers do, too."

Tommy paused and turned to her. "I know what you meant about being a helper for Jesus, Mother. I guess I don't have to wait till I grow up."

"You're a very wise young man," Tommy's mother praised him.

That night, after he had said his prayers, Tommy remembered the day. He could still remember the sweet smile on his baby sister's face when he had tied her shoe, and Mrs. Brown's smile when they had helped her with the groceries. And, he was glad he'd made a new friend because he had learned to share his ball glove. Tommy went to sleep with a smile on his face. It was sort of fun being a helper for Jesus.

I Need Your Help, Lord

by Frances Carfi Matranga

I pray, O Lord, You'll bless me
And guide me every day;
I want to please You, Father,
In all I do and say.

But oftentimes I stumble;
I'm selfish and unkind.
And then I feel so sorry,
So troubled in my mind.

I really need Your help, Lord;
Please keep me 'neath Your hand
Until I meet You face to face
Within the promised land.

Bear and Owl Think About Trust

by Julaine Kammrath

"Oh dear, oh dear, look at the ground," complained Bear nosing a crevice of snow. "I remember this stuff. My mother took me out in it when I was a cub. Now I'm by myself, and when the cold comes, I won't find enough food. Oh, Owl, I'll die!"

"No you won't, Bear," said Owl. "You will sleep all winter and not need much food at all."

"Are you sure?" asked Bear.

"Trust me. I know about these things," answered Owl.

"But, Owl, how will I stay warm in winter if I'm not moving around?"

Owl looked at his friend and smiled. "Why, Bear, all that fat and fur will keep you cozy."

"Are you sure?" asked Bear.

"Trust me. I know about these things," answered Owl.

A light snow began filtering down through the trees. Bear padded over the dry pine needles, making a muffled crunch-crunch in the stillness. After a while Bear stopped and slowly looked around. "Where have all the bears gone? Am I the only one left?"

Owl settled on a broken branch in front of Bear. Tenderly Owl said, "There will be other bears about in the spring. You will find a friend."

"Are you sure?" asked Bear.

"Trust me. I know about these things," answered Owl.

Owl remained on the branch cleaning his feathers while Bear moved on. Several hours later, Owl spotted Bear sitting in a clearing. Owl hooted a greeting to Bear, who was looking anxiously around.

Adapted from material in *Jesus My Friend,* Eternal Word ® Kindergarten Teachers Guide. Copyright © 1984 Concordia Publishing House.

"Owl, Owl, I can't find anywhere to sleep!" called Bear.

Turning back, Owl flapped into the clearing.

"I've been searching and searching. I can't find any place where the snow doesn't keep twitching my nose!" whimpered Bear.

"We will find a place together then," said Owl.

"Are you sure?" asked Bear.

"Trust me. I know about these things," answered Owl.

So Bear and Owl searched for a sleeping place. When they found a dry cave, Bear snuggled down and closed his eyes. Just as Owl was about to fly away, Bear whispered, "Oh, dear Owl, what if you aren't here when I wake up?"

"I will be here, Bear."

"Are you sure?" asked Bear.

"Trust me. I know about these things," answered Owl.

Bear nodded sleepily, "Good night then, Owl."

"Good night, Bear."

"I love you, Owl."

"And I love you, Bear."

The Talents of Bear

by Julaine Kammrath

The rushing stream pushed against Bear's paw as he hunted for fish. In the stillness Bear heard the throaty whistle of a robin.

"Oh, listen! I do think robins have the loveliest voices. I wish I could sing like that!"

Bear lifted his head to the bird and sang, "Ba-a-a-awl!" But the bird shuddered and quickly flew to a different bush. Bear dropped his nose and mumbled, "But I can't."

Sniff, sniff, sniff. Bear smelled something and he turned around.

"Oh, look! I do think deer are the most graceful animals. There's a mother doe with her fawn. They move so smoothly. I wish I could move gracefully like that!"

Bear lumbered toward the deer. Rumply, rumply, rumply, rumply. The startled deer leaped quickly away. Staring at the empty spot, Bear murmered, "But I can't."

Suddenly something flashed by overhead. Bear climbed a tree for a good look.

"Oh, stop! Let me fly with you! Geese have such strong wings and they fly so fast. I wish I could fly like that."

Bear looked at his front legs and began flapping them up and down, up and down. The tree limb quivered and finally cracked. Down fell Bear with a thump. Rubbing a sore paw, Bear sighed, "But I can't."

A large tear rolled down Bear's face and plopped to the ground. "I can't do anything," he sobbed, "nothing at all." Bear hunched against the tree and cried and cried.

Adapted from material in *Jesus My Friend,* Eternal Word ® Kindergarten Teachers Guide. Copyright © 1984 Concordia Publishing House.

When Bear was quiet again, he heard someone calling, "Bear! Bear!" Bear wiped his nose and said, "Who's calling my name?"

"I'm up here, Bear. Look up!"

Bear shook the tears out of his eyes and peered up at his friend, Owl. "Oh, sniff, hello, Owl. I'm feeling very sad. The robins sing so wonderfully, but I can't. And the deer move so gracefully, but I can't. Geese fly so swiftly, but I can't. Oh, Owl, I'm not special at all." And Bear broke out in fresh tears.

"Now, now, Bear. Let's have none of that sorry-for-myself crying. Rattle those good brains of yours, and let's put our heads together." Owl flew down from the tree and perched on Bear's shoulder.

"Tell me, Bear, what were you doing when you heard the robin?" asked Owl.

Bears think slowly, so it was a little while before Bear said, "I was fishing and then—"

Owl interrupted. "What was that again?"

"I was fishing."

"Fishing—and how did you know those deer were nearby then?" asked Owl.

Bear paused again. "Well, I smelled them."

"Oh, you can smell animals from a distance. And what were you doing when you tried to fly?" asked Owl.

"Well, I climbed the tree and—"

Owl interrupted again. "Oh! You climb trees too! You can fish, smell, and climb trees! Well, well, well. What a remarkable fellow you are!"

Slowly a smile spread across Bear's face. "That's true, isn't it! I can do things! Am I special then, Owl?"

"Yes," answered Owl. But you're special to me for a different reason."

"What's that, Owl?" asked Bear.

"Because I love you."

And Bear's eyes sparkled.

Somebody Loves Me

by Frances Carfi Matranga

Somebody loves me,
I can't help but know;
Somebody's with me
Wherever I go.
Somebody truly
    and really cares
And lovingly listens
    to all of my prayers.
He's somebody faithful;
He's somebody true—
The Father in heaven,
He loves me—and you!

Faithful Servant

by Tellie Hart

Rebekah wiped sweat from her forehead onto the shoulder of her dress as she worked in the cooking shed attached to the house. She turned the fish in the frying pan which was over the fire. A spatter of grease on her hand made her cry out in pain. She quickly looked into the house toward the bedroom.

"Are you all right, Girl?" called a woman.

Rebekah hurried to the bedroom door. She put on a smile as she entered. "Just hot mutton grease spatter."

The woman pushed back the quilt and moved to sit up. "You're such a little girl to be preparing a meal alone. I'll come and help." She stood a moment, teetering.

Rebekah rushed to her. "Oh, Naomi, please get back into bed." She gasped, "Oh, you're so hot! Perhaps I should go and find the physician."

"No," protested Naomi weakly. She allowed the girl to tuck the quilt over her again. "Peter said he was going to invite the Master and some of His men for supper. There's so much to do! Will you bring me a cold, wet cloth for my head? I'll be all right soon and come to help you."

Rebekah laid the damp cloth on Naomi's forehead. She heard the sigh of relief, then returned to the cooking shed.

Smoke! The fish in the frying pan! She rushed to take the pan from the fire. "Oh!, ouch! The pan's hot!" Quickly, Rebekah set it down upon the stones and plunged her hand into a pan of cold water. Oh, how it hurt!

She glanced into the house again toward the bedroom, afraid that Naomi had heard her cry of pain. There was no sound. What if she saw the smoke curling all through the cook house? Rebekah grasped a towel and flapped at the smoke, driving it outside. A gentle breeze assisted her, and soon the house was free of smoke.

Rebekah sank upon a small stool to examine her sore hand. Blisters were forming. Pain crept up her arm. She blinked back the tears. There was no time to waste. The men would be coming soon. Her heart sank at the thought of what Naomi's son-in-law, Peter, might say if the meal was not prepared. He was always so gruff. Only with Naomi was he gentle. Rebekah could wrap her hand later. There was too much to do right now.

"Be sure to wash the greens to remove all the sand," Naomi had cautioned. "The loaves are made and ready, and there's a melon cooling in a pan of cold water. Set the table for about ten. Andrew will be here, too, and I don't know how many Peter will bring after the synagog service."

Rebekah hurried to fry some more fish. The first ones were burned black. She would eat those herself. She ignored the pain in her hand. A blister had already broken. She winced, but she must hurry to get everything done.

Once she had seen and heard the Master. What had He said on that mountain? "Blessed are the poor in spirit, for theirs is the Kingdom of Heaven." Well, if anyone was poor, she certainly was, but she could see no sign of any Kingdom of Heaven. Where was it?

She would not even have a home except for Naomi, who had come to Rebekah the day her mother had died. She comforted Rebekah and insisted on bringing her back home with her. Rebekah bit her lip. The least she could do would be to become a helpful servant in Naomi and Peter's home.

Rebekah was frightened of Peter. One day, while he was gone to the seashore to repair his fishing nets, Naomi had tried to explain. "Don't worry about him, Dear. Peter's just that way. Under all that bluster he is really a very

162

kind person. He's a sad person, too. It's hard for a man to watch his wife die."

"But he never smiles!"

Naomi nodded wisely. "Perhaps he has his reasons. Life is a serious matter to him. He has been wonderful to me, of course. How many men would give their mother-in-law a good home after their wife died? He takes good care of me . . . just like a son, you know."

Now Rebekah hurried to the long wooden table with a stack of bowls. She stumbled. One of the bowls crashed to the dirt floor. It hit a small stone and fell into pieces. Now she had awakened Naomi again! Tears welled up in Rebekah's eyes as she hurried to the bedroom door to explain. Naomi lay unmoving upon the bed, eyes still closed. The damp cloth had fallen to the floor. Oh, her face was so red! She was very sick!

Just then Rebekah heard voices outside. The men were coming! Hurry! Pick up the pieces and get another bowl! She rushed around.

They were talking as they entered. "Did you see that rabbi's face when Jesus told the unclean spirit to come out of that man? It was purple, I tell you!"

Rebekah looked up. Yes, there He was. The Master looked different up close like this.

Peter caught her eye and frowned. "Where's Mother?" he asked.

Rebekah nodded toward the bedroom. "She's not feeling well, but supper is almost ready. It will only be a few minutes."

She stopped in surprise at the sight of men entering Naomi's bedroom. Why had Peter taken them in there? It was unseemly. Even a small girl knew that.

Rebekah's hand throbbed as she carried the large kettles to the table. She sniffed away the threatening tears. She was arranging the loaves on a platter when Naomi entered. "Here, let me help you, Child," she said cheerfully. "How can I thank you for all you have done?"

"Why, you're up!" gasped Rebekah. "You were so very sick, but now you look fine."

Naomi smiled down at her. "It was Jesus who healed me. I'll tell you all about it later. Right now, let's feed these hungry men." She took the platter from Rebekah. "You look all worn out, Child. Let me do that. Sit down and rest. I'll serve the men."

Rebekah gratefully sank onto the stool. She watched Naomi hurry back and forth with food. Now that Rebekah had stopped working, the pain in her hand was almost more than she could bear. She gripped her wrist, looking at the huge blisters. Too stiff with sore muscles to move, she was still sitting there when she heard the men push back their chairs. The meal was over.

She was startled to see Jesus coming toward her. He smiled, taking her hand in His. His eyes noted the tear stained cheeks. He spoke softly.

"That was a delicious dinner, my child. Well done, good and faithful servant."

When He rejoined the men in the other room, Rebekah was so thrilled to have been touched by the Master, by the One who had healed her Naomi, that the pain in her hand seemed to be gone. Even the blood in her veins seemed to sing with joy.

Was He, Himself, then, the Kingdom He had talked about?

Switch

by Chris Youngman

"Why do I have to go to bed now?" Tommy howled. "Greg stays up later."

"I'm older than you," his brother Greg said smugly. "I'm in sixth grade, and you're only in first."

"That's enough, boys," their mother said. "You have to go to school tomorrow, Tommy, and it is bedtime."

Tommy stomped off to his room. On the way, he picked up his white cat, named Jaws. "Greg thinks he's so smart," Tommy said to the purring animal. "He can go downtown with his friends. He can play outside longer at night. He can stay up later. But I'm not little any more. I'm not in Kindergarten. We're both in the same grade school!"

When he reached the door of his room, he heard Greg and his mother laughing. "They're laughing at me!" Tommy said, slamming his door.

Tommy's mother came to tuck him into bed. "How would you like to play a game tomorrow?" she asked.

"What game?" he asked with a frown.

"You can be Greg for tomorrow," his mother answered. "Whatever he does, you can do."

Tommy looked at her. "Can I stay up later?"

"As late as Greg does," she said.

The frown changed to a smile. Tommy bounced in bed. "I can hardly wait!" he shouted.

"We'll start as soon as you get up," his mother promised. "Now it's time to say your prayers and go to sleep."

But Tommy stayed awake a long time, planning. "This is going to be fun!" he told Jaws, who was curled up on his quilt.

The next morning, Tommy woke up happy, but slightly tired. He dressed quickly and went to the kitchen.

"I'm Greg today," he reminded his mother. "I'm ready for breakfast."

"Good morning, Greg," his mother smiled to Tommy. "I go to work early today. You know what that means."

Tommy had forgotten that Greg made breakfast when their mother had to leave early.

She said, "Have a good day, Tommy—I mean, 'Greg.' I'll be home when you get back from school." The door closed behind her.

His brother came into the kitchen. "I'm Tommy today," he said. "Where's breakfast?"

Tommy put bread in the toaster. It burned while he poured milk. Some spilled, and Jaws jumped up on the table to lick it up. She left milk tracks along the table. Tommy ran to get some paper towels. While wiping up the milk, he knocked over the cereal box. He started to ask Greg for help, but saw his older brother grinning at him. Tommy decided he could do it himself.

Tommy was so busy cleaning up after breakfast that he arrived at school hot and breathless, just in time for the bell. "At least I can play later tonight," he thought as he slid into his seat.

After school, Tommy was ready for his snack. Then he changed clothes and went out to play.

Tommy and his friends liked to play in Sue's backyard. It had a treehouse, lots of space to play ball, and trees to climb. Sue, Tommy, and two of their friends played until supper time.

Tommy walked home, thinking of all the fun he would have after supper. His mother met him at the door. "I'm glad you're back," she said. "Please set the table."

"But that's Greg's job," he answered before he remembered.

Tommy almost broke a glass. He put the knives and forks on the wrong sides of the plates. He forgot to put the salt and pepper on the table. By the time everything was done, his feet were dragging.

They had a small pie for dessert. Tommy's mother always cut pie so there was a small extra piece. The extra piece was always for Tommy. But today, just as Tommy reached for his second piece, Greg snatched it away. "I'm Tommy today," he reminded his younger brother.

Tommy glared at Greg, but before he could say anything, his father spoke. "Greg," he said, looking at Tommy, "I have to clean the garage this evening. I need you to help."

Tommy was speechless. He wanted to go out to play again. And now he had to help clean a dusty, cluttered old garage! After watching Greg eat his pie!

Cleaning the garage was hard work. Tommy's hair hung in his eyes, and he left a greasy smudge on his face as he brushed the hair out of the way. His arms hurt from lifting cans of paint, tools and boxes. He sneezed from all the dust he had raised while sweeping. Finally they were done, and Tommy could go.

At Sue's yard, everyone was leaving. "I have to go home now," Peter said.

"My mother wants me to come in," Sue said.

"It's getting dark," Sarah added, waving good-bye.

It was no fun for Tommy to stay out when none of his friends could play with him. He started home, head hanging and feet shuffling.

"Back already?" his mother asked.

Blinking his eyes to hold back tears, Tommy said, "I want to be Tommy again. It's no fun being Greg. It's too hard."

"Fine," said his mother. "If you're Tommy again, it's time for bed."

Tommy opened his mouth to argue, then closed it again. He and his mother looked at each other. Then they both started laughing.

His mother hugged Tommy. "You will be older before you know it," she said. "God has planned growing so that every age is just right for learning a little more before you go on to the next stage."

"When I say my prayers, I'll ask Jesus to help me remember that," Tommy said. "And, I'll ask Him to forgive me for being jealous of Greg."

"That's a good idea," his mother answered. "Remember, it's fun—and not too hard—to be twelve when you *are* twelve."

A Thank-You Prayer

by Gloria A. Truitt

Thank You, Lord, for summer rain
    That gives the earth a drink;
For family love and hours of play
    And quiet times to think.
Thank You for my food and clothes—
    All things that You provide.
But most of all, I thank You, Lord,
    For being at my side.

Tulips of Love

by Guin Dyer Calnon

Katrinka's wooden shoes felt as light as two flower petals as she scurried from her garden and ran toward her cottage home in Holland.

"Mama, Mama," she shouted, swinging open the door. "My tulips are coming up. I've counted five of them now!"

"I'm happy for you, Darling. Remember to keep giving them the best care. This has been an unusually dry spring."

"Oh, I will, Mama. Every day I'll water them. I can't wait to enter them in the contest. How many more weeks is it, Mama?"

Her mother reached over and gave her a hug. "Just eight more, Dear."

Katrinka picked up her sprinkling can from the window sill and skipped back outside. After giving each sprout a hearty drink, she sat down on a nearby rock. How exciting it would be to win first prize for the most beautiful tulips! Visions of brightly-colored tulips seemed to dance before her, and she could almost feel the judge pinning a blue ribbon on her dress.

Each of her classmates had similar dreams as they tended their gardens. This was the highlight of the spring season for every fourth-grader in the village.

On the way to school the next morning, Katrinka hurried down the street, anxious to tell her best friend, Gretel, about her five little seedlings. "I wonder how many have come up in Gretel's garden," she thought as she skipped along the familiar path.

Approaching their meeting place, Katrinka looked as far down the road as she could, but her friend was nowhere in sight. As she waited, she watched the ripples twirling endlessly in the canal off to the side of the road. What fun it would be to let her shoe bob up and down on those tiny waves!

She slipped it off and set it lightly in the water. As though eager to receive it, the current caught it and playfully carried it down the canal. Her lace cap fluttering in the breeze, she walked along the edge of the dyke, following her wooden vessel. What fun it was! Just like sailing her own little boat on a miniature lake.

All at once, a strong wind blew, pushing her wooden shoe out toward the middle of the canal.

"Oh, no! Come back, come back!" Katrinka called. She knelt down and stretched as far as she dared over the edge of the dyke, but she was unable to catch her shoe. On it went as though it were determined to reach the other side. Desperately she looked around for a stick, but could find none. Then she remembered the time. "What am I going to do? I've got to get my shoe back, or I'll be late to school. I wonder where Gretel is."

Running over the cobblestones, she took one last look to see if her friend was coming; but the road was still empty.

"Please, God," she prayed silently, as she hurried back to the canal, "make the wind send my shoe closer to the bank." But, when she neared the canal, it was nowhere in sight.

"Katrinka!"

Hearing her name, she turned, hoping to see Gretel. Instead, she faced Willem, a classmate who lived close by.

"Hi, Willem," she greeted him, trying to be pleasant. "Have you been fishing this morning?"

"I was—until something better came along."

She followed his gaze to the wooden shoe spinning from the end of his pole. "Oh, there's my shoe!" Katrinka exclaimed, thankful to see it was no longer in the canal.

"*Was* your shoe," Willem snapped back with a smug expression on his face.

"Please let me have it, Willem." She stepped toward him.

"Well, come and get it." He turned and strode off in the opposite direction.

Katrinka hurried after him, but soon Willem was running. She pulled off her other shoe and began to chase him. "Please give it to me!"

"Come and get it; come and get it," Willem continued to shout. He walked to the brink of the canal and, swinging his fishing pole, let Katrinka's shoe dangle precariously over the water.

"Stop, Willem!" Katrinka cried, rushing after him. "I want my show, now!"

"You can have it—if you can reach it." He leaned lazily against a tree and watched a bird fly by.

Catching him off guard, she grabbed his pole toward her and let go, sending her shoe flying through the air.

"Ooww!" Willem winced as the pole sprang back and snapped hard against his forehead.

She darted past him and retrieved her shoe at last. "There! I got it from you, so you needn't think you're so smart." She slipped both shoes on her feet and headed down the path toward the school.

"Just because you won this time, don't think you can win the tulip contest, too," he shouted after her, rubbing his head with the palm of his hand.

"I'm certainly going to try," Katrinka stopped long enough to answer. "Five sprouts have already come up in my garden."

"Well, don't count your tulips before they've bloomed," Willem retorted, strutting down the path behind her.

All day Katrinka kept watching for Gretel to arrive, but her desk remained empty. After school, Katrinka stopped at her friend's house.

"Please come in, dear," Gretel's mother greeted at the door. "Gretel will be very glad to see you. The doctor says she needs rest and is to stay in bed for several weeks. She's physically run down again."

"Several weeks!" whispered Katrinka in dismay. "Oh, I hope it won't . . . " She stopped short when she came to the bedroom. There she saw her friend, weak, lying on her pillow.

"Hi, Gretel. I sure missed you today. I'm sorry you're not well."

"I'm glad you came, Katrinka. Did anything exciting happen at school?"

"No, it was just a usual day. Please try to get well fast. I hope it won't take as long as the doctor thinks."

"I *will* try hard. I want so much to take part in the tulip contest." Gretel swallowed hard as her eyes filled with tears. What would happen to her tulips if the drought continued, with her confined to her bed, unable to care for them? She tried to put the thought out of her mind. "Have any of your tulips come up yet?"

"Yes, five sprouts came up yesterday." Then Katrinka quickly added, "Maybe you'll be able to enter after all. Let's pray that Jesus will heal you soon, if it's His will." She reached over and held Gretel's hand. As she finished praying, she paused, then added, "And if it's not Your will, Lord, let something good come from this so that we all might be drawn closer to You. Amen."

"I'd better run on home, Gretel, but I'll stop by each day after school and bring your assignments to you."

Katrinka slipped out into the back yard and toward the flower garden. Poor Gretel; not even one shoot had come up yet. If only there were something she could do to help her. "I know what I'll do," Katrinka said. "I'll surprise her by taking care of her garden. Then, if she's not well, I'll enter her flowers in the contest for her." The more Katrinka thought about it, the more enthused she became.

One afternoon, as Katrinka neared her friend's garden, two sprouts were peeking their heads above the ground. It was exciting to see results at last. Each day thereafter, both Katrinka's and Gretel's gardens continued to prosper.

The day before the festival, Katrinka greeted Gretel with exuberance. Although she knew Gretel would not be well enough to attend the festival, she thought of how surprised her friend would be when she heard her tulips were there. Afraid to stay any longer lest her secret should slip out, she turned to leave.

"Be sure to tell me everything that happens, Katrinka."

"Oh, I will." Katrinka's long braids bounced about as she jumped down the steps. In the morning she would come back to pick up Gretel's flowers.

She skipped along while singing her favorite spring song of the dancing tulips, dressed in their magnificent gowns, curtsying to one another. Pretending she was a tulip, she went prancing over the cobblestones, swinging her head from side to side. As she ended her little show with a curtsy and raised her head, there to her surprise stood Willem.

"What are you so happy about?" he snapped.

"Tomorrow's the Tulip Festival. Aren't you excited, too?"

"Why should I be? What's so good about a Tulip Festival, anyhow?"

"You know you want to win just as much as everyone else," she said with a saucy toss of her head.

"Well, if anyone wins, it won't be you. I'll see to that."

"Your threats don't scare me, Willem!" She turned and struck up the tulip waltz again as she merrily made her way home.

When she arrived, she ran to her tulip garden. How beautiful the flowers were, swaying in the breeze, their brightly colored heads bending this way and that.

"Oh, it's so hard to choose which flowers to take," cried Katrinka. "They look like they belong in a queen's garden." Her eyes scanned the rows of velvet reds and purples, deep pinks and cheery yellows. "I'll wait and pick them in the morning," she decided. "That way they'll be fresh."

Katrinka walked over to her favorite rock and sat down. It was too lovely an evening to go inside so soon. She would stay out and enjoy the beauty of the flowers.

Gradually the sun lowered. The brilliant colors of the tulips faded and revealed a new beauty as they were silhouetted against the sunset sky, ever spinning as if refusing to give up their frolicking.

Through the past few weeks a bond had grown and flourished between Katrinka and her tulips. She felt each flower was sharing her excitement, spilling over with laughter and gaity, knowing that the new day would bring the thrill of the annual festival. It would be their hour to show forth their exquisite beauty.

"They must be as delighted as I am to be in the festival," she thought.

At last the tulips grew still as if aware that they would need some rest before the next day. "Sleep well, my pretty ones," she whispered, bending over the drowsy tulips.

As she made her way to the house, a shadow crossed her path. In the darkness, something ducked behind a bush. While she stood, peering through the night, a dog rushed out at her and began to growl.

"Why, that's Willem's dog," she said, feeling sure she knew what had caused the shadow. "Hi, little pal. Don't you remember me?" She leaned down to pet the dog, but he lunged at her, growling louder. "I don't believe you do remember me. If you don't want to be friends, I'll just say good night." As she walked away, he continued to snap at her heels.

"I'm glad he's not my dog," she thought as she sliced a large ball of cheese for supper that evening.

The next morning, Katrinka sprang from her bed. At last the big day had arrived! She ran outside, ready to pick the twelve loveliest blooms. Running toward her garden, she strained her eyes to see. Something was wrong! Where were all the velvet heads that always beckoned to her? Not a single flower stood to greet her.

Upon reaching the garden, her eyes fell to the ground. Trampled petals of every hue lay scattered over the soil. Her body became rigid as she let out a scream. "Ohhh, nooo! What's happened to my tulips! Mama, Mama!" Bursting into tears, she ran blindly toward the house.

Hearing Katrinka's cry of alarm, her mother hurried from the cottage and caught her daughter in her arms. "What's the matter, Dear?"

"Ohhh, Mama! Just look at my garden! Every tulip is crushed. Completely destroyed! How could this have happened?" She broke into fresh sobs. "Now what can I do?"

"Darling, Jesus knows all about it. Even though it seems like a disaster to us, He will use it for His purpose." She drew Katrinka's head on her shoulder and held her close.

"I don't even want to go to the Tulip Festival, now. Everything's ruined! How could any good come from something so evil?"

"Katrinka, we'll just have to wait for the Lord to show us."

"It's impossible! I'm not going! Why should I, when I have nothing to take?"

She slipped from her mother's arms and ran into the house. Burying her face in her pillow, she cried till she was exhausted.

Suddenly, she sat up with a start. "I know just what I'll do, and no one will ever know. Why didn't I think of it before?" She ran to the basin and splashed cool water over her face. It would never do to let anyone see that she had been crying.

Hurrying as fast as she could, she stumbled over the cobblestone street and nearly lost her balance. Never had the stones seemed so treacherous. Slipping and stumbling, at last she came to Gretel's house and slid through the open gate and back to the garden. Looking around to make sure no one was watching, she quickly clipped twelve of the prettiest flowers nearest her. As she finished, she looked about once more. No—no one had seen her.

She crept back out of the yard and continued down the road. What a lovely bouquet the tulips made! But they didn't make her the least bit happy. And their pretty heads hung as if they had lost their joy, too.

"Well, why shouldn't I enter them as my own?" she tried to convince herself. "I did all the work, didn't I?"

Gretel's words rang in Katrinka's ears: "I want so bad to take part in the Tulip Festival . . . be sure to tell me everything that happens." Katrinka remembered how Gretel's lip had trembled as she began to speak, and how she had lowered her head and blinked back a tear when she had finished. Gretel had missed all the fun of caring for her garden and seeing the stages of growth of each tulip. "And now I'm depriving her of her only part in this event. Oh, poor Gretel. How can I do this to you, my best friend? How could I have even considered taking your tulips as my own?"

She set the flowers aside and sank down by the canal. "Dear Jesus, forgive me for ever wanting to do something so heartless. Cleanse my heart, Lord. Help me to think of others and not just myself."

As she opened her eyes, they fell on the tulips. "It no longer matters whether I win first place." She felt free and joyful as she picked them up. Even the tulips seemed to sense her change of heart as their heads bounced about while she carried them home.

"Mama, I'm going to the Tulip Festival after all," Katrinka cried as she darted through the open door.

"Where did you find your lovely tulips, Dear? I thought they all were destroyed."

"These are Gretel's, Mama. I'm entering them for her."

"Darling, you've already won. You've won the greater victory by your spirit of Christian love. Katrinka, Dear, you are offering tulips of love."

"That's sweet, Mama. Now I understand what you meant. Jesus has used all these events for His purpose— to draw me closer to Him and to make me more loving toward others."

She gave her mother a big hug and flew out the door. If she hurried, she could still make it before the festivities began.

She was out of breath as she reached the front of the assembly and handed her bouquet to one of the judges.

"And what is our final contestant's name?" he asked as he took them from her with a smile.

"Oh, these are my friend's, Gretel de Vries. She's not well, so I'm entering them for her."

As she turned to find a seat in the audience, she spotted Willem in the front row and smiled at him. Avoiding her eyes, he began to scrutinize the hat he held in his hand.

After a lot of preliminaries, the judges finally came to the part for which Katrinka had been waiting.

"And now, for the third place winner, . . . " Katrinka focused her attention on the judge, " . . . we have Wilhelmina Koornstra. Second place goes to Gretel de Vries; and the first place winner is none other than Willem Van Hooks!"

Cheers rang out while the air filled with Dutch caps belonging to every boy assembled on the front lawn of the school.

Then, just as suddenly as the cheering had begun, it stopped.Low whispers could be heard everywhere—which gradually increased in volume. Looks of shock and unbelief were seen on all the children's faces.

Surprised at the change of response, the judge raised his hand. "Boys and girls, something is obviously amiss. We will all be silent and let one student be the spokesman for the group."

A hush fell over the gathering as the judge looked from one student to another. "Does no one have anything to say?" he asked.

As if drawn by a magnet, all eyes turned on Willem.

"I do, Sir," Willem began as he stood to his feet. "I have not earned first place, and everyone knows it. Those aren't my tulips. My garden was ugly. Nothing would ever grow in it." He hung his head as if hesitant to go on. "I was jealous of Katrinka because she had the most beautiful tulips I'd ever seen. I was determined she would not get first place, so I destroyed all her tulips with the help of my dog. But, before I did, I gathered some of the best ones to enter as my own. I've done a wretched thing." He paused and covered his face with his hands. Everyone was surprised; Willem had never said anything like that before.

"I probably wouldn't have confessed, but when I saw Katrinka care enough for someone else to win although there was no chance of her winning, for the first time in my life I realized how selfish I was." He faced the group, a look of relief on his face. "All I ask is for each of you to forgive me—but, especially you, Katrinka."

As Willem sat down, the judge stood silent for several moments. "What we've seen today took a great deal of courage. I think this has made an impact on all of us.

179

Because Katrinka sowed a seed of love, it spread to Willem and, continuing to blossom, it has touched us all."

The judge paused for a moment and went on. "As I'm sure you are all aware, there is a change in the final winner. Our first place winner for the most elegant tulips is Katrinka Van Veen. Will the two winners present please come forward to receive your awards."

"How wise Mama is!" Katrinka thought as she made her way home that morning. The words kept going through her mind, "Darling, Jesus knows all about it. Even though it seems like a disaster to us, He will use it for His purpose."

As she fingered the beautifully carved pendant of three tulips in full bloom, she whispered, "Lord, let me always be willing to give tulips of love to others."